A

FINDING WONDER

Way

AND MEANING

With

IN THE LANGUAGE

Words

OF LIFE

JOHN C. BOWLING

Beacon Hill Press of Kansas City
Kansas City, Missouri

Printed in the
United States of America

Cover Design: Paul Franitza

Library of Congress Cataloging-in-Publication Data

Bowling, John C., 1949-
    A way with words : finding wonder and meaning in the language of life / John C. Bowling.
      p.   cm.
    Includes bibliographical references.
    ISBN 0-8341-1802-5
    1. Christian life.   I. Title
   BV4501.2.B682   1999
   248.4—dc21
                                         99-13413
                                       CIP

10   9   8   7   6   5   4   3   2   1

This book is respectfully dedicated to
the students of Olivet Nazarene University
whose many conversations with me
have enriched the wonder and meaning
of my life. All proceeds from this book
will go to student scholarships.

Mrs. Jordan —
with love and
respect —
John B Lyg

CONTENTS

INTRODUCTION

Words are the raw material of language, the building blocks of communication. Dictionaries are filled with words —but it's how these words are used that makes the difference.

Words hurt; words heal.
Words break; words bind.
Words create and nurture.
They soothe and encourage.
Words instruct us
and correct us
and inspire us to lives of meaningful service.

Words have both the explosive power of dynamite and the comforting effect of oil on troubled waters. Words sung to a child in a quiet song at bedtime can bestow peace and rest; words spoken in anger and passion can bring forth violence and destruction. Truly we must choose our words well, for they carry great power.

One of the first things noted in a general semantics course is that the word is not the thing—that is to say, a word, the collection of letters and sounds, is different from the thing it represents. The word *dog* is not the same thing as the flesh-and-blood animal that runs to see you or barks at strangers. While this is true, there is a reality to words and the effects that result from their use and abuse.

Words are more than just symbols of something else— they are instruments of creation, creating a reality of their own. The Hebrew term for *word* is *davar,* which also means *thing.* This underscores the fact that while a word represents a real thing, it is also a real thing itself.

Just as we must learn to arrange the alphabet into words, we must also learn to arrange the words of our lives into sentences and paragraphs of personal meaning—words not written or audible, but words lived. Life takes on depth and character as we learn to translate each word we use into the unspoken language of everyday life.

This book is a collection of essays wherein a series of words is brought to life. This is not a vocabulary list but a litany of some of life's most trenchant words. These words have been selected not from a dictionary but from life itself.

Each word can be a telescope to see beyond ourselves and a microscope for looking within. These essays are both windows and mirrors. This book is a tool to assist you to come to terms with life, one word at a time. The goal is understanding, wisdom, and faith.

Three things must occur for the power of a word to become reality for an individual. He or she must see the word, hear the word, and say the word.

Seeing the word is more than noting its construction and learning the letters that give it form. To see a word is to have some picture, some experience, some image of the word coming to life. It is at this point we become aware that such a word exists.

The first time I remember seeing *charity* was one night as a child when, from the backseat of our old Chevy, I watched my father and mother deliver groceries to a family in need. This became a common sight for me as I was growing and learning the vocabulary of life.

I saw the word *courage* not long ago as a disabled student came forward to receive his graduate degree. He left his wheelchair at the far end of the platform, and when his name was called he hobbled across to shake my hand and receive his diploma. Just after he got past me he fell, and several of us rushed to help him up, only to hear him say, "I can do it." Without any assistance, he picked himself up and completed his minimarathon to the cheers of a standing ovation.

Once you see a word, it begins to take on a life of its own, and you seek to know more about it. You want to hear it for yourself.

Hearing the word is to learn what it means, its intricacies and implications and how it is to be applied. The question that *hearing* asks is not so much "What does this word look like?" but "What does it mean?" Why were my folks taking food from our cupboards and giving it away?

Next, for the word to become a living part of your life, it must be said not just with voice but with action and passion. **Saying the word** is to cross the bridge of application, to put the word to use in your life.

I remember learning to say the word *work* when I took my first summer job. I learned how to work, how to recognize and then analyze a job to be done, and how to follow through. I learned that work is hard but that there is a joy to it. It calls for discipline but also brings a sense of worth and accomplishment.

Words are not magic, but they can be magical. The Aramaic for "I create as I speak" is *Avara k'davara* or in the language of the magician, *Abracadabra.* Words make things happen.

Many of the great ceremonies and rituals of life are ceremonies of words as well as action. It is with words that marriages are established, degrees are awarded, contracts are fashioned. We use words as we name our children and say good-bye to our parents. Nations are bound together with words woven into treaties. It is with words that we declare our faith and our doubts.

For words to retain this kind of power, they must be personally renewed from time to time. Words, old and new, can get worn by overuse or dusty from neglect. Meanings can change with time, and even the most powerful words can lose their force if misused or used too often. This book seeks to dust a few of these off and hold them up to the light, so as to catch the wonder and depth of their original meaning and their abiding potency.

Just as there is a spiritual dimension to all of life, there is a spiritual element in each of these words as well. God certainly has a way with words. "God said, 'Let there be light,' and there was light" (Gen. 1:3). God made the world with words, and words continue to be instruments used of God to create and re-create, to fashion and form us into His likeness.

J. I. Packer observed, "Keys open doors; keywords open minds, and through minds hearts." May the words that follow provide the keys to a more meaningful living conversation with life.

Almighty God, bestow upon us the meaning of words, the light of understanding, the nobility of diction, and the faith of the true nature. And grant that what we believe we may also speak.

—Hilary (A.D. 315-67)

Success
is not a
harbor,
but a
voyage.
—Richard M. Nixon

Success

A favorable or desired outcome. Accomplishing what is attempted. An effort that turns out well.

SEEING THE WORD . . . *SUCCESS*

His name was Don, and he showed up at my office unannounced one summer afternoon. I greeted him, and we talked about 40 minutes, after which we parted, both having a better understanding of success.

"How can I help you?" I asked.

He told me he was 35 years old and that he had worked as an appliance repairman for the past 15 years. "I like it and I'm good at it, and I have some great friends at work, but I think I ought to go to college," he said.

When I asked him why, he told me that although he liked what he was doing, he felt that he had gone about as high with his company as he could. "If I'm going to get ahead, I think I need a college education."

I quizzed him for a few minutes, "What do you mean by 'get ahead'?" I asked.

"You know," he said.

I nodded. "What would you like to do if you could do something else?"

"I'm not sure."

"Tell me about your family."

"I have a great wife and two young children. We're getting along OK, and I'm very happy at home."

I talked to him about what it would take to start college from scratch at his age. If he quit work and went full time, it would take him 4 years. If he went part time, it could take as long as 10 years. I talked to him about the option of earning an associate degree at the community college. We talked about the financial cost involved.

"Don, it won't be easy, but I'm confident you can do it if you really want to," I said. "What do you really want in life? What do you want from your future?"

He replied, "What I really want in life is a happy family, enough money to live on, and a job I like and some good friends."

As he finished that sentence, we both smiled. He already had what he wanted. He had just lost sight of it for a time.

"Don," I said, "you're already a success."

We talked a little longer and agreed that he would enroll for a course at the community college and pursue some additional education, a little at a time, for the simple joy of learning.

HEARING THE WORD . . . *SUCCESS*

What is it to achieve success? In any activity? In life itself?

One of the most common maladies of our time is a misunderstanding of success. Bookstores and library shelves are filled with books on "how" to be successful, yet

I fear we have thought little about what true success really is, what it requires of us, and what its rewards and disappointments are.

Many people labor under false ideas of success. As a result, they never find it, or if they do gain what they have sought, it becomes an empty reality. Henry Ward Beecher spoke of false, fleeting success like this: "Success is full of promise till men get it; and then it is last year's nest from which the birds have flown."

Genuine success, however, is not an empty promise, a false hope. True success fills a person with deep feelings of fulfillment, happiness, and joy.

But how do you define success?

Can you be successful without being wealthy?

Mother Teresa certainly lived a life of great success, and yet she owned almost nothing. I know folk who have great success at gardening, homemaking, and service to others—for which they earn no money. Our idea of success should never be confused with our idea of wealth.

Can you be successful without being well known?

For many, to be successful is to be famous. Ask a hundred individuals to list 10 successful people, and most will name the rich and famous. Success, however, is one thing; fame is another. Think of how many well-known individuals from the world of sports or business or entertainment there are whose lives have disintegrated in spite of their apparent "success."

Can you be successful without having power or social status?

My friend Don, the appliance repairman who loves his work and his family, would say yes. And so would I.

You can be successful with or without wealth, fame, power, or social status. Success is measured not by those false standards but by the happiness and joy that come as you fulfill the deep longings of your spirit.

Authentic success is not just money in the bank, but a contented heart and peace of mind. Success is feeling good about who you are. It comes when you value *being* more than *doing.*

Success itself can never stand alone as the goal of life. To seek true success is to seek to attain the goals we believe are most deeply right for us. Therefore, success is not possible without a proper sense of the meaning of life, which involves having the right goals backed up with the proper values.

Jesus said it best of all: "What good will it be for a man if he gains the whole world, yet forfeits his soul?" (Matt. 16:26).

The most successful people are those who love what they do, do it well, and love those with whom they live and work. They live not just for themselves but for God and the good of others. This success is open to all regardless of wealth or social status. It flows from being true to yourself and being good to others.

Henry David Thoreau said, "If one advances confidently in the direction of his dreams and endeavors to live the life which he has imagined, he will meet with success unexpected in common hours."

Saying the Word . . . *Success*

We all want to be successful—and we *can* be once we understand the true nature of success.

Success should not be limited to one area of your life—success at work, for example. Rather, it should considered in light of all facets of your life: as wife or husband, as friend, parent, son or daughter, citizen, neighbor, worker, and so on.

Success is making the most of your total self. It is as much process as product. It involves making the most of your hours, days, weeks, months, relationships, and tasks. You must determine what success is to you. Without this personal understanding, you will constantly be trying to measure up to someone else's standard.

It's true that success does not come easily. There are often many failings along the way, yet success flows from getting up just one time more than you fall down. Success seems to be largely a matter of hanging on after others have let go. Remember: there's no traffic jam on the extra mile.

What are your goals in life?

What is the measure of success in your life?

What does success look like when you picture it in your mind?

PRAYER

O God, there is no ultimate success apart from You, and with You in my life there can be no ultimate failure. Help me to give myself to the things that really count for success and to avoid chasing after the many impostors that are presented to me daily. In Jesus' name. Amen.

We should not let our fears hold us back from pursuing our hopes.

—John F. Kennedy

Hope

To desire with anticipation. To expect with confidence. A desire accompanied by an expectation of fulfillment.

SEEING THE WORD . . . *HOPE*

The plane, on a war mission in the Pacific, had been forced to ditch into the open sea, and for eight days the flight crew had been drifting helplessly without food or water. Their faces were burned, their mouths and bodies parched. The heat, hunger, and exhaustion had brought them close to the breaking point.

The captain, Eddie Rickenbacker, had been in dangerous situations before. He alone refused to despair. He never gave up hope that they would be rescued.

One of the men had a small Bible, and throughout those first few days Rickenbacker had the men take turns reading it aloud. It provided reassurance that they were not alone.

By the eighth day the men were desperate. There was no sign of a boat, no sound of a plane, no sight of land—nothing but the wide, empty, rolling sea. As it came time for the scripture to be read that day, this passage from Matthew was selected:

> Take no thought, saying, What shall we eat? or, What shall we drink? or, Wherewithal shall we be clothed? . . . for your heavenly Father knoweth that ye have need of all these things.
>
> But seek ye first the kingdom of God, and his righteousness; and all these things shall be added unto you.
>
> Take therefore no thought for the morrow: for the morrow shall take thought for the things of itself *(Matt. 6:31-34, KJV)*.

In a newspaper story that appeared from coast to coast, Rickenbacker told what happened next:

> Were it not for the fact that I have seven witnesses, I wouldn't dare tell this story because it seems so fantastic. Within an hour after the prayer meeting on the eighth day, a sea gull came out of nowhere and landed on my head. I reached up my hand very gently and got him. We wrung his head, feathered him, carved up his carcass and ate every bit, even the little bones. We distributed and used his innards for bait.
>
> Captain Cheery caught a little mackerel about six or eight inches long, and I caught a little speckled sea bass about the same size, so we had food for a couple of days. . . . That night we ran into our first rainstorm. Usually you try to avoid a black squall, but in this case we made it our business to get into it and catch water for drinking.

The men drifted for nearly two more weeks and were then finally rescued. "I consider the story of how we prayed and how our prayers were answered the most important message I ever gave to the people of this country," Rickenbacker said.[1]

HEARING THE WORD . . . *HOPE*

It has been said and often repeated that "where there is life there is hope." While there is a measure of truth in that axiom, it takes on a deeper meaning when it is reversed: "Where there is hope there is life."

It is hope that gives vitality and power to life.

Hope spurs us to get up when we have fallen,
to continue when we are tired,
to try once more when we have failed,
to believe in the face of doubt,
to light a candle in the dark.

Hope never sounds retreat. It revives ideals, renews dreams, revitalizes visions. Hope scales the peak. It wrestles with the impossible. It is the miracle medicine of the soul.

Emil Brunner, a Swiss theologian, said, "What oxygen is for the lungs, such is hope for the meaning of life." The spiritual asphyxiation of our time is the result of a profound lack of hope.

Hope is one of the three great pillars of the Christian life. It is on hope, along with faith and love, that the whole of Christian experience rests. Only a Christian can be an optimist regarding the world. Only a believer can cope effectively with life, and only one with hope of eternal life can face death with peace and confidence.

Christian hope is not simply a trembling, hesitant wish, a kind of "cross your fingers" faith. Rather, it is the confident expectation that even if all else fails, God, and all His promises, are trustworthy and solid.

Hope is not wishful thinking, cheery optimism, or even

a deep yearning. Hope is a gift of God through Christ, which produces a confident, unshakable trust in His faithfulness and a vibrant expectation that His gracious promises will be fulfilled.

Hope is the fruit of faith.

"We have this hope as an anchor for the soul, firm and secure" (Heb. 6:19). What a rich metaphor this sentence provides, assuring us that our faith and God's faithfulness give us hope for the storms of life! In the fierce winds of adversity and the turbulent waves of doubt, we can have a sure and steadfast anchor.

The top end of an anchor line secured to a ship is called the "bitter end." Imagine the panic you would feel if you were at anchor during a storm and suddenly saw the "bitter end" slipping across the deck and down the side of the hull into the sea. That must be the way many people feel as they face life without being securely tied to the anchor.

Saying the Word . . . *Hope*

People are hopeless because they hope in the wrong things. They cast about for something visible, tangible, material on which to pin their hopes—real estate, precious metals, stocks and bonds, position, power, prestige, popularity—then suffer when it fails.

The scripture speaks to this by teaching us that "what is seen is temporary, but what is unseen is eternal" (2 Cor. 4:18). Obviously, hope in the temporary is doomed. When such hope dissipates, it leaves behind frustration and emptiness.

In the Bible, "hope" is most frequently used as a noun rather than a verb: something we possess, as opposed to something we do. It is a gift from God. It does not flow from a self-generated optimism.

God has given the human family a hope that is the fulfillment of everything else we long for: security, happiness, love, acceptance, prosperity, freedom—these are all fulfilled in the kingdom of God. Hope is therefore dependent on Jesus and His work. Christian hope is not founded on anything that humanity has done, or can do, for itself. It is founded on what Christ has done for us.

Authentic hope must have an ultimately reliable source. It must be able to sustain us in all of life's circumstances and answer our questions about our present times in the light of the end times. Only Jesus can give that kind of hope. Therefore, consistent, lasting hope is a relational dynamic that comes from a personal, intimate trust in the One in whom we live and move and have our being (Acts 17:28).

Hoping is not dreaming. It is not spinning an illusion of fantasy to protect us from our boredom or distract us from our pain. Hope is a confident, alert expectation that God will do what He has said He will do. It is imagination put into the harness of faith. It is the opposite of making plans that we demand God put into effect, telling Him both how and when to do it. Rather, it is a willingness to let Him do it His way and in His time.

When you face a difficult situation or a problem that seems to have no answer, consider again God's promise: "I know the plans I have for you, says the Lord. They are plans for good and not for evil, to give you a future and a hope" (Jer. 29:11, TLB).

You *can* trust in God. As the storm clouds gather, check your anchor and be assured that God's protective, enabling, and sustaining grace will see you through.

To strengthen your confidence this week, read the following verses each day as a "refresher of hope":

No one whose hope is in you will ever be put to shame. . . . Show me your ways, O LORD, teach me your paths; guide me in your truth and teach me, for you are God my Savior, and my hope is in you all day long.

—Ps. 25:3-5

We wait in hope for the LORD; he is our help and our shield. In him our hearts rejoice, for we trust in his holy name. May your unfailing love rest upon us, O LORD, even as we put our hope in you.

—Ps. 33:20-22

Why are you downcast, O my soul? Why so disturbed within me? Put your hope in God, for I will yet praise him, my Savior and my God.

—Ps. 42:5-6

Find rest, O my soul, in God alone; my hope comes from him. He alone is my rock and my salvation; he is my fortress, I will not be shaken.

—Ps. 62:5-6

The LORD delights in those who fear him, who put their hope in his unfailing love.

—Ps. 147:11

Those who hope in the LORD will renew their strength. They will soar on wings like eagles; they will run and not grow weary, they will walk and not be faint.

—Isa. 40:31

Everything that was written in the past was written to teach us, so that through endurance and the encouragement of the Scriptures we might have hope.

—Rom. 15:4

Lay hold upon the hope set before us: which hope we have as an anchor of the soul, both sure and stedfast.

—Heb. 6:18-19, KJV

PRAYER

My Lord Jesus, I beseech you, do not be far from me, but come quickly and help me, for vain thoughts have risen in my heart and worldly fears have troubled me sorely. *How shall I break them down? How shall I go un-hurt without your help?*

I shall go before you, says our Lord; I shall drive away the pride of your heart; then shall I set open to you the gates of spiritual knowledge and show you the privacy of my secrets.

O Lord, do as you say, and then all wicked imaginings shall flee away from me. Truly, this is my hope and my only comfort—to fly to you in every trouble, to trust steadfastly in you, to call inwardly upon you, and to abide patiently your coming and your heavenly consolations which, I trust, will quickly come to me.[2]

—Thomas à Kempis

*Attitude,
rather than
circumstance,
sets the tone
of life.*

Gratitude

Appreciation for kindness or benefits received.

Seeing the Word . . . *Gratitude*

Every Sunday afternoon for many years William Waffles, a Methodist pastor in Ohio, would go to a nearby prison to conduct services and visit with the men who were incarcerated there. During these visits, a trusting and loyal relationship developed between the pastor and his prisoner parishioners.

For some time, the pastor and his wife had been saving for a trip to the Holy Land. On the Sunday afternoon before they were to leave, he shared with the prisoners his plans. "We've worked hard and saved and finally this lifelong dream will soon be ours," he told them. "I won't see you for a couple of weeks." He assured them of his prayers and concern, even though he would be away.

The prisoners were delighted for him. They immediately gathered around him and hugged Rev. Waffles, patted him on the back, shook his hand, and jostled him lovingly with much attention and camaraderie.

A little later, as the pastor was getting ready to leave, one of the prisoners awkwardly came forward with a package that had been hastily wrapped with a single strand of ribbon. The fellow said, "We didn't have time or money to get you a gift, but we wanted you to think of us while you are away, and this is the best we could do. Please don't open it 'til you get home. Then, when you open it, remember—it's all we had to give you."

The pastor thanked them, prayed for them, and took the package home. He told his wife how pleased the men seemed to be about the trip and how they had given him this gift. She, too, was delighted and watched intently as he opened the package.

Inside he found his wallet, his pen, his watch, his glasses case, and his pocketknife. What had happened was this: when the prisoners had gathered around him to offer their congratulations, they had picked his every pocket. And then wrapping it all up, they gave it back to him as a sign of their love, saying, "It's all we had to give."[1]

HEARING THE WORD . . . *GRATITUDE*

That's our story too. We've all picked the pockets of God. Paul asks this question in 1 Cor. 4:7, "What do you have that you did not receive?"

All of life is a gift from God. Yet many of us hold on to our possessions and talents and opportunities as if they were really ours instead of His. We could take a lesson from those prisoners—wrap up with the ribbon of devotion the things we have received, and give them back to God through love and service.

Once we become convinced of this principle—that all we have we have been given—attitudes about life and possessions begin to change.

For example, English scholar Matthew Henry was once robbed of his wallet by a pickpocket. This is what he wrote in his diary that evening:

Let me be thankful. . . .

First, because I was never robbed before;

Second, although he took my wallet, he did not take my life;

Third, because, though he took my all, it was not much; and

Fourth, let me be thankful because it was I who was robbed, not I who robbed.[2]

That's a remarkable attitude, one that rests upon an understanding that all of life is a gift.

The psalmist said it well: "Praise the LORD, O my soul; all my inmost being, praise his holy name. Praise the LORD, O my soul, and forget not all his benefits. . . . For as high as the heavens are above the earth, so great is his love for those who fear him" (Ps. 103:1-2, 11).

There's great freedom for us once we adopt a deep and genuine attitude of praise and thanksgiving about life. The incidental things and the disappointments and hurts of life, which so often rob us of joy, have a way of dissipating as we "forget not all his benefits."

Corrie ten Boom, reflecting on life's struggles, said, "Don't wrestle—nestle." What freedom is ours as we learn to rest in the Lord, rejoice in His presence, give thanks for His gifts, and invest our lives in His service.

SAYING THE WORD . . . *GRATITUDE*

Attitude, rather than circumstance, sets the tone of life. Thus, the scripture says, "Give thanks in all circumstances" (1 Thess. 5:18). This attitude of thankfulness transforms an individual from the inside out. It instills a positive outlook and imparts a resiliency that enables a person not only to face life but also to overcome it with joy.

This attitude is cultivated as you take time to count

your blessings. Say the word just now by making a list of the things, aspects, and people in your life for which you have genuine gratitude. Express your gratitude to God and to the people in your life who help to enrich it, remembering that

All we have, we have been given.

All we are, we are in Christ.

All we do, we must do for God.

"Let the peace of Christ rule in your hearts, since as members of one body you were called to peace. And be thankful" (Col. 3:15).

PRAYER

O God of grace, every good and perfect gift comes from You. Accept my thanks for who You are and for Your daily blessings upon my life. Even in the midst of difficulty, I am grateful that You have promised to work in all things for my good. Truly, You are gracious—You are good. In Jesus' name. Amen.

> *Adversity has made many a man great who, had he remained prosperous, would only have been rich.*
>
> —Maurice Switzer

Adversity

A condition of suffering or affliction. A disastrous experience; calamity.

SEEING THE WORD . . . *ADVERSITY*

It was a gray dawn on April 9, 1945, in which German theologian and pastor Dietrich Bonhoeffer was executed in a concentration camp at Flossenburg, Germany, by special order of Heinrich Himmler. The charge against him was treason. For Bonhoeffer, however, his resistance to Nazism was an act of obedience to Jesus Christ.

Bonhoeffer was 16 when he chose to study for the ministry. By the age of 21 he presented his doctoral dissertation for approval. In 1928-29 he served as assistant pastor for a German-speaking congregation in Barcelona, Spain. The next year he traveled to America to study at Union

Theological Seminary in New York City. He returned to
Germany in 1931 to teach systematic theology at the University of Berlin.

In 1933 Hitler and the National Socialist Party came to
power. Young Bonhoeffer recognized the danger inherent in
this development and began to resist the growing influence
of the Nazis. By 1938 he was forbidden to teach or write or
publish and was identified as an enemy of the state.

While visiting America in 1939, he was advised not to
return to Germany. War seemed imminent, and his personal safety appeared at risk. However, he felt compelled to return and be a part of the struggle of his people. He was
eventually imprisoned and finally executed only weeks before the arrival of the Allies.

One of Bonhoeffer's last letters from prison contained
this prayer:

O Lord God, great distress has come upon me;
my cares threaten to crush me, and I do not know
    what to do.
O God, be gracious to me and help me.
Give me strength to bear what thou dost send,
and do not let fear rule over me;
take a father's care of my wife and children.
O merciful God, forgive me all the sins
that I have committed against thee and against oth-
    ers.
I trust in thy grace and commit my life wholly into thy
    hands.
Do with me according to thy will and as is best for me.
Whether I live or die, I am with thee,
and thou, my God, art with me.
Lord, I wait for thy salvation and for thy kingdom.
    Amen.[1]

There is no easy explanation for the why, where, or
when of adversity. It is often a soul-wrenching experience,
yet when Christ enters into these moments of affliction,
there is hope and the grace of endurance.

HEARING THE WORD . . . *ADVERSITY*

Thomas à Kempis wrote, "It is good for us at times to have troubles and adversities; for often they make a man enter into himself, so that he may know that he is in exile, and may not place his hopes in anything of this world."[2]

Adversity does not mean that God has abandoned us or that we're being singled out for punishment. Some forms of misfortune come as a direct result of our actions. The person who smokes for 40 years may be forced to face the rigors and pains of lung cancer. But most cases of personal adversity are inadvertent. Adversity is not to be viewed as a penalty or consequence. Christ himself was innocent but yet afflicted.

Although the role of adversity in God's plans and purposes cannot be fully understood, we can be assured that "in all things God works for the good of those who love him, who have been called according to his purpose" (Rom. 8:28).

Adversity is a good test of a person's resiliency, of his or her ability to cope, and ultimately of his or her faith.

A father took his young son out into the country for his first rifle practice. The son raised the gun and fired as his father had instructed him. The blast of the gun nearly scared the boy out of his wits, and the powerful recoil of the rifle threw him backward into his father's arms. Anticipating this very thing, his father had taken a position behind his son to catch him. It was with a new appreciation for his father that the boy pulled himself together again.

Life is like that. The shock of some experience unnerves us, and the recoil throws us backward. That is, it *seems* that it's backward. But when we find ourselves in the arms of our Father, who was waiting to catch us and support us, we discover that it's a forward experience.

Paul knew something of adversity. He spoke of his "thorn in the flesh" and prayed to God repeatedly for its removal. But God didn't remove it. Instead, He gave Paul this gift of assurance: "My grace is sufficient for you, for my power is made perfect in weakness" (2 Cor. 12:9). So Paul could assert, "I consider that our present sufferings are not worth comparing with the glory that will be revealed in us" (Rom. 8:18).

SAYING THE WORD . . . *ADVERSITY*

How are we to respond when adversity comes? Although adversity is a painful pedagogue, there are lessons to be learned that may not be grasped in any other way. James writes, "Consider it pure joy, my brothers, whenever you face trials of many kinds, because you know that the testing of your faith develops perseverance. Perseverance must finish its work so that you may be mature and complete, not lacking anything" (James 1:2-4).

Perhaps Job, the Old Testament character who lost nearly everything that was precious to him, provides the best way to respond to adversity. Scripture records, "In all this Job did not sin nor charge God with wrong" (Job 1:22, NKJV).

- Job held steady to his belief in God.
- He resisted the negative opinions of others.
- He resisted both accepting blame for his adversity and placing the blame on others.
- He patiently endured and learned lessons he would otherwise never know.
- He came to the right conclusion: "Shall we indeed accept good from God, and shall we not accept adversity?" (Job 2:10, NKJV).

The truth is, bad things do happen to good people (and bad people as well). We must recognize that we live in a fallen world and that we will all have to face our share of adversity. The question is not "Will I suffer some loss or pain?" but rather "How will I respond to the inevitability of adversity?"

In dealing with adversity, you should prepare in advance by

- recognizing the reality and certainty of some share of adversity. Don't be surprised—be prepared.
- developing your relationship with and reliance on God throughout the course of daily life. Establish your life on a solid foundation before the storms come. Don't ask God for immunity but for strength and grace to bear whatever may come.
- establishing a support system of friends and family to whom you can turn in need. The church is a great source of help in times of trouble.

As adversity comes, accept it, commit it, hold steady, seek counsel and support from others, and draw strength from God. The Lord is at work in your life in the midst of difficulty. This is clearly proclaimed in Isa. 43. Note the key word "through," which is repeated in these verses. This indicates that we will come out on the other side of the adversity, for God is with us:

Fear not, for I have redeemed you; I have summoned you by name; you are mine.

When you pass through the waters, I will be with you; and when you pass through the rivers, they will not sweep over you. When you walk through the fire, you will not be burned; the flames will not set you ablaze. . . .

You are precious and honored in my sight, and . . . I love you. . . .

Do not be afraid, for I am with you *(Isa. 43:1-2, 4-5)*.

Albert Camus observed, "In the midst of winter I finally discovered within me an invincible summer."

PRAYER

Holy Spirit, turn for us life's disappointing setbacks into experiences that move us forward spiritually, through Christ, whose cross was turned into a crown. In Jesus' name. Amen.

Life itself is a prayer, and the prayers we say shape the lives we live, just as the lives we live shape the prayers we say.

—Ted Loder

Prayer

A devout petition to God. Spiritual communion with God, including adoration and supplication.

SEEING THE WORD . . . *PRAYER*

At St. Catherine's Monastery near Mount Sinai in Egypt rests a strange pair of caskets. Several centuries ago two young men who were part of that monastic community took a vow. They pledged to one another and to God to devote their lives to perpetual prayer and adoration.

It was their intent to spend every moment of every day of every week and month and year in praise and prayer. To accomplish this vow, they were assigned to adjoining rooms and were fastened together at the wrists by a length of chain.

The plan was for one to pray and the other to sleep and vice versa. From the moment they began, they neither saw nor spoke to each other again. Their only contact was the chain that ran through the wall.

When one was finished with his prayers, he would tug on the chain to awaken the other. A tug back meant that the other had begun and the first man could rest. Back and forth they prayed for decades until they died. In honor and remembrance of their devotion, their remains lie side by side in caskets still united by the same chain.

This is a remarkable story of commitment, devotion, and determination, but it misses the point of prayer. It's true that God calls us to a life of devotion, obedience, and prayer, but these obligations should not be viewed as chains that bind us. Prayer is intimacy with God. It is building and maintaining a vital spiritual relationship. As we pray, we have the assurance from God's Word that He hears our prayers. This is affirmed clearly in the Scriptures: "Does he who implanted the ear not hear? Does he who formed the eye not see?" (Ps. 94:9) and "Before they call I will answer; while they are still speaking I will hear" (Isa. 65:24).

HEARING THE WORD . . . *PRAYER*

To pray is to know God. The true aim of prayer is to know God. Too often we focus narrowly on our petitions and intercessions and lose sight of this primary purpose.

My wife, Jill, and I are bound together by a covenant we made years ago to each another. The "chain" that binds us is not burdensome, for it is our love for each other. Our conversations are the natural expression of that relationship.

I don't wait to talk with Jill until I need her help with something. I talk with her because I love her, and the needs have a way of being cared for as a natural part of loving conversations.

These conversations take different forms. Sometimes they're joyful conversations whose sole purpose is to simply enjoy each other's presence. Sometimes our conversations focus on particular issues. Sometimes they're brief, sometimes long. Sometimes they're filled with laughter, at other times with tears. But each conversation deepens and enriches the relationship. Prayer is similarly the conversation of a loving relationship.

Jesus demonstrated and taught us about this personal aspect of prayer when He said to His followers, "When ye pray, say, Our Father which art in heaven" (Luke 11:2, KJV). The first words of prayer are words of relationship: *Our Father.* Prayer is to build and strengthen that relationship.

Prayer is not an exercise in which we try to get God's attention or talk Him into something. It is spending time with Him. Prayer really makes sense only in terms of relationship and against the backdrop of God's nature.

- It is because God is holy that we must confess.
- It is because He knows everything that we must and can be totally honest before Him. We can tell God anything and everything.
- It is because He is sovereign that we must ask according to His will.
- It is because He is loving that we come to Him as Father.

As we come to know God through prayer, we also come to know ourselves more fully.

To pray is to know oneself. Prayer has a way of uncovering and refining us. God doesn't simply respond to our prayers—He responds to us, to our whole life. What we say to God in prayer cannot be isolated, segregated from what we think, feel, will, and do in the other moments of life. Prayer is communication from whole persons to the wholeness of God. It is much more an opportunity than an obligation.

My dad is a busy man. He still runs a large business with scores of employees and many obligations. Like most executives, if he is to give his time and energy to the most important tasks, he must have help screening his calls. Some inquiries must be directed to others who can be of assistance.

So if you were to call my dad's business some morning and ask for my father, a secretary would answer. She would ask if she could help you or if she could direct your call to someone else.

But what if *I* were to call my father? The secretary would answer, and I would say, "I'm calling for Mr. Bowling, please. This is his son, John."

She would reply by saying, "Your dad's in a meeting, but I know he'd want to talk to you. Hold for just a moment." The next voice I would hear would be that of my father.

In the same way, no one's voice sounds sweeter to God than yours. Nothing in the cosmos would keep Him from directing His attention to your prayers.

If imperfect fathers love to bestow blessings on their children, imagine how our perfect Father in heaven must delight in giving good gifts to us, His children.

SAYING THE WORD . . . *PRAYER*

"We must never wait until we feel like praying before we pray for others. Prayer is like any other work; we may not feel like working; but once we have been at it for a bit, we begin to feel like working."[1]

There may be no more fitting image to express the intimacy with God that can occur in prayer than the image of God's breath. We are like asthmatic people who are cured by the breath of God. The Holy Spirit brings new life and energy as we pray. Prayer is God's breathing in us.

Do you regularly take time to take a deep breath of God? Just as in the physical or athletic world, as the labor gets more difficult, our breathing becomes more intense. Just so, when we are tempted, tried, or tested, let us breathe deeply.

PRAYER

Dear listening God, grant me the ease to breathe deeply and unhurriedly in this moment of prayer. Help me to see You more clearly and understand Your ways more fully.

Give me ears to hear You clearly. Give me eyes to see Your hand at work in the world, in my world. And give me a heart quickened by Your Spirit, so that it beats in rhythm with the very heart of God.

Teach me to pray, even as I pray. In Jesus' name. Amen.

*Just as courage
takes its stand
by others "in"
challenging
situations, so
compassion
takes its stand
"with" others in
their distress.*

—William J. Bennett

Compassion

A feeling of deep sympathy and sorrow for
someone struck by misfortune, accompanied by
a desire to alleviate the suffering.

SEEING THE WORD . . . COMPASSION

The late Margaret Mead, a well-known anthropologist, was asked on one occasion what marked the earliest sign of civilization in a given culture. The questioner expected the answer to be a clay pot or perhaps a primitive tool. Dr. Mead replied, "A healed femur."

She explained that no healed femurs are found where the law of the jungle—the survival of the fittest—reigns. A broken leg that has been healed shows that someone cared for the injured person. Somebody had to do the injured person's hunting and gathering until the leg healed. So, Mead suggested, compassion is the first sign of civilization.[1]

Compassion is a sure sign of godliness as well. Compassion is God at work through us, and when compassion is extended to one in need, God is present in that moment.

Jesus put it like this:

A man was going down from Jerusalem to Jericho, when he fell into the hands of robbers. They stripped him of his clothes, beat him and went away, leaving him half dead. A priest happened to be going down the same road, and when he saw the man, he passed by on the other side. So too, a Levite, when he came to the place and saw him, passed by on the other side. But a Samaritan, as he traveled, came where the man was; and when he saw him, he took pity on him. He went to him and bandaged his wounds, pouring on oil and wine. Then he put the man on his own donkey, took him to an inn and took care of him. The next day he took out two silver coins and gave them to the innkeeper. "Look after him," he said, "and when I return, I will reimburse you for any extra expense you may have."

Which of these three do you think was a neighbor to the man who fell into the hands of robbers?

The expert in the law replied, "The one who had mercy on him."

Jesus told him, "Go and do likewise" *(Luke 10:30-37).*

HEARING THE WORD . . . *COMPASSION*

God is not a distant God, existing solely at arm's length from the human struggle. No, Scripture declares, "They will call him 'Immanuel,'—which means, 'God with us'" (Matt. 1:23).

When we begin to see God as Immanuel, we recognize that He has committed himself to share in our pain as well as in our joy, in our failures as well as in our days of triumph. The God-with-us is a close God—a refuge, a stronghold, an "ever-present help in trouble" (Ps. 46:1). We can never fully appreciate the compassionate nature of God if we do not understand what John was telling us as he wrote, "Christ . . . lived here on earth among us" (John 1:14, TLB).

What was He like as He lived with us? He was compassionate and kind, slow to anger, and abounding in love. We need to pay close attention to Jesus' words and actions if we're to gain insight into the nature of divine compassion. He reached out, He reached down, to the poor, the ignorant, the sinful, the sick, the hungry, the blind, the lonely— He cared (and still does) for us all. And then He said, "Go, and do thou likewise" (Luke 10:37, KJV).

Compassion is a feeling of deep sympathy and sorrow for someone struck by misfortune. It is accompanied by a desire to alleviate the suffering. Compassion is the child of love and a first cousin to mercy.

In a scene from Charles Dickens's famous holiday story, *A Christmas Carol,* Scrooge is visited by the ghost of his departed partner, Jacob Marley. Marley appears wearing a great chain. As he addresses Scrooge, he begins to lament how he lived:

"No space of regret can make amends for one's life opportunities misused. Such was I, such was I."

"But you were always a good man of business, Jacob," faltered Scrooge, who now began to apply this to himself.

"Business!" cried the Ghost, wringing its hands again. "Mankind was my business. The common welfare was my business; charity, mercy, forbearance, and benevolence were, all, my business. The dealings of my trade were but a drop of water in the comprehensive ocean of my business!"

Marley says it very well—caring for others is our business.

SAYING THE WORD . . . COMPASSION

Compassion asks us to go where it hurts, to enter into places of pain, to share in brokenness, fear, confusion, and anguish. It requires us to be weak with the weak, vulnerable with the vulnerable, and powerless with the powerless.

"Do we look at the poor with compassion? They are hungry not only for food; they are hungry to be recognized as human beings. They are hungry for dignity and to be treated as we are treated. They are hungry for love."[2]

A twofold calling is associated with being compassionate. First, we must ourselves be strengthened and encouraged by the compassion of God: "As a father has compassion on his children, so the LORD has compassion on those who fear him; for he knows how we are formed, he remembers that we are dust" (Ps. 103:13-14).

Second, we are then to be compassionate to others in need. Just as compassion marks the character of God and the ministry of Jesus, it must also be reflected in the people of God: "Therefore, as God's chosen people, holy and dearly loved, clothe yourselves with compassion" (Col. 3:12).

Compassion is not among our most natural responses. We are pain-avoiders by nature, at least until our nature is changed by the compassionate One.

Can you think of someone you know who is bereaved?

Do you know someone who is ill?

Is there a person in your circle of influence who is discouraged?

What can you do *today* to show the love of Christ to those in need?

PRAYER

Merciful God, You know our weakness and distress. Yet the weaker we are, the stronger is Your help. Grant that we may accept with joy and gratitude Your greatest gift of compassion: He who dwelt among us, and dwells among us still, through His Holy Spirit.

May we bear witness to Your work in our lives through our work in the lives of others. In Jesus' name. Amen.

Never give in, never
give in, never,
never, never, never
—in nothing, great
or small, large or
petty—never give
in except to
convictions of
honor and good
sense.

—Winston Churchill

Perseverance

Persistence. Continuing in spite of counter influ-
ences, opposition, or discouragement. Steadfastness.

SEEING THE WORD . . . *PERSEVERANCE*

At the end of May each year, a green flag drops at the
Indianapolis Motor Speedway signaling the start of the
world's most celebrated automobile race. Thirty-three
gleaming turbocharged cars shoot out of the fourth turn
and roar past the starting line at over 200 miles per hour.
What a sight!

On the pace lap and the first few racing laps, every car looks great and runs strong. However, people who follow "Indy" every year understand that the goal is not just to start well but to finish well.

Give the race a little time, and, as in every year, a toll will start to be taken. Engine failure, tire problems, and a host of other calamities will befall car after car until perhaps as many as half of the drivers who started the race will fail to finish it.

It's hard to overemphasize the importance of finishing well. Trophies rarely get handed to those who cross only the starting line of a race. The prize and the money go to the ones who cross the *finish* line.

HEARING THE WORD . . . *PERSEVERANCE*

Perseverance pays. It is a costly investment of will and effort, yet it pays great dividends. Most great accomplishments would never have come to pass without the will to persevere. David Livingstone, the great missionary doctor, said, "I will go anywhere as long as it is forward." That kind of commitment is at the heart of perseverance. There may be many times in life when we give out because of fatigue or other stress, yet we need not, we must not give up.

United States President Calvin Coolidge said it well: "Nothing in the world can take the place of persistence. Talent will not; nothing is more common than unsuccessful men with talent. Genius will not; unrewarded genius is almost a proverb. Education will not; the world is full of educated derelicts. Persistence and determination are omnipotent. The slogan 'press on' has solved and always will solve many of the problems of the human race."[1]

Perseverance is not just a personality trait that some exceptional people have—it's a spiritual grace and virtue that all of God's children may possess. Perseverance does not rest on self-sufficiency but rather on being "God-sufficient." Paul confidently stated, "I can do everything through him who gives me strength" (Phil. 4:13).

SAYING THE WORD . . . *PERSEVERANCE*

The August 1991 issue of *Runner's World* told the story of Beth Anne DeCiantis's attempt to qualify for the following year's 1992 Olympic Trials marathon. A female runner must complete the 26-mile, 385-yard race in less than two hours and 45 minutes to compete at the Olympic Trials.

Beth started strong but began having trouble around mile 23. She reached the final straightaway at 2:43, with just two minutes left to qualify. Two hundred yards from the finish line, she stumbled and fell. Dazed, she stayed down for 20 seconds. The crowd yelled, "Get up!" The clock was ticking—2:44, less than a minute to go.

Beth Anne staggered to her feet and began walking. Five yards short of the finish, with 10 seconds to go, she fell again. She began to crawl, and with the crowd cheering her on, she crossed the finish line on her hands and knees. Her time? Two hours, 44 minutes, 57 seconds.[2]

What does it take to finish *your* race—your career commitments, your family priorities, your faith commitments?

You must commit yourself to the task. I like Paul's phrase from the Bible in which he speaks about the race of faith and simply says, "Let us run with perseverance the race marked out for us" (Heb. 12:1) and his admonition to "run in such a way as to get the prize" (1 Cor. 9:24).

Every racer at the Indianapolis 500 knows what it means to run in such a way to get the prize:

1. *No one wins who does not enter.* One might be the best race car driver the world has ever seen, but the racer will not win unless he or she races. Everything else flows from that point of entering.

2. *Each driver must stay on course.* The race is a 500-mile race, but that doesn't mean that a driver can drive from Indianapolis to Louisville and back and expect to win the prize. It's not a race of 500 miles in any direction. It's not 500 miles in a straight line.

It's a race over a prescribed course, and if one does not stay on course, he or she can't win the race.

3. *The driver also knows that he or she must follow the rules of the race.* One cannot suddenly decide to go the opposite direction on the oval track, or perhaps stop in the middle of turn three to stretch his or her legs or check the oil. These things will lead to disqualification (or worse). The rules are not there to hamper the race but to enhance it. Enter the race, stay on course, obey the rules, and watch for the checkered flag.

4. *The driver must watch for the checkered flag.* You run better when you keep the goal always before you.

The race is not to the swift, nor to the strong, but to the faithful. "He who began a good work in you will carry it on to completion until the day of Christ Jesus" (Phil. 1:6).

Remember: perseverance pays!

PRAYER

O God, Author and Finisher of the faith, help me, through Your grace, to finish what You have started in me.

Give me strength when I'm weak,
courage when I'm frightened,
peace when I'm troubled,
faith when I doubt, and
courage under fire.

You, who never give up on me, help me never to give up on You.

Help me fix my gaze not on what is seen but on what is unseen. "For what is seen is temporary, but what is unseen is eternal" [2 Cor. 4:18]. Surely Your grace is sufficient, and Your power is made perfect in weakness.

I am confident, for I am Yours. In Jesus' name. Amen.

*We don't go
to church or
have church
or build a
church. We are
the church.*

Church

The called-out ones.

SEEING THE WORD . . . *CHURCH*

Early in our ministry my wife, Jill, and I had the privilege of pastoring a wonderful church in Dallas. When we left there, the ladies of the senior adult group gave us a lovely quilt they had made. The name of each person who worked on it is stitched into it.

Each year as the weather turns cool, we pull out the blankets and quilts, and with that one particular quilt comes a flood of wonderful memories. Just seeing those names brings to mind stories of lives that were woven together with our lives for a time. Although we have been separated now from that place and those folks for years, the memories and the bond are still there.

Among the names on that quilt are those of two sisters, Babe and Fannibelle. In all the time I was there, I never discovered Babe's real name. Everyone just called her "Babe."

I confess I felt more than a little strange one Sunday as I was escorting a denominational leader to the platform for the morning service. We passed this lady in the foyer, and she smiled and said, "Hello, Pastor."

I said, "Good morning, Babe."

The visiting clergyman just looked at me as if to ask, "Why are you calling this woman 'Babe'"?

The writing on the quilt is not just names—they're people, each one with a story. Those individuals, different one from another in so many ways, have became one people, a family, the church.

I hosted a dinner one evening with a very special group of university students, missionary kids from around the world. We went to a local restaurant and were seated at one large table. When we were all in place, I looked at them gathered all around the table and said to the group, "This is like having dinner with the Waltons." We laughed a bit and began to get acquainted.

After we knew each other a little better, one of the students bravely asked, "Dr. Bowling, who are the Waltons?"

These students were raised in Africa, South America, Asia, and India. They had politely laughed at my comment, but they had no frame of reference by which to know what I meant. So I took a moment to tell them about *The Waltons* television series and all the imagery of family life that now accompanies that surname.

Then I talked with them about the church. I told them that although they were thousands of miles from their moms and dads, they were now very much a part of our local church family. They had a place at the table—they belonged.

HEARING THE WORD . . . *CHURCH*

"The Church of Jesus Christ, older than any university, dynasty, or government, is the most significant institution of society. Indeed, even as the Bible is the best of books, the Church is more than the best in any list of social institutions.

Created by grace and headed by Christ, the Church is Spirit-led, worships God in Word and sacrament, engages itself with the Great Commission, and is uniquely significant."[1]

Today's dictionaries begin their definitions of the word *church* with these words: "a building for public and especially Christian worship." It is an unfortunate development that the idea of *church* is now primarily *building*. In the Bible, *church* does not mean a building but a people.

The Greek New Testament word for *church* is *ekklesia,* which means "the called-out ones." The Church is the people of God, called out from the world around them. "Once you were not a people, but now you are the people of God; once you had not received mercy, but now you have received mercy" (1 Pet. 2:10).

As the people of God, the Church is a community of believers, a fellowship that is both human and divine, both visible and invisible, temporal and eternal. The Church exists for worship, witness, service, nurture, and fellowship.

Throughout the New Testament, a variety of images are used to describe the Church: "the Bride of Christ," "the family of believers," "God's household," "vineyard," "field," and "living stones." The most frequent metaphor is "the Body of Christ," appearing 19 times.

This image suggests many things. It speaks of both the unity and the diversity of the Church. Paul writes, "Now the body is not made up of one part but of many" (1 Cor. 12:14), and then goes on to say of the Church, "Now you are the body of Christ, and each one of you is a part of it" (v. 27).

The "Body" metaphor also underscores that the Church is not to be viewed as an organization, in a social or political sense, but as an organism, a living entity. The people of God comprise a kind of embodiment of Christ in whom He lives and moves and ministers throughout the world.

Hans Kung observes, "The Church is always and everywhere a living people, gathered together from the peoples of this world and journeying though the midst of time. The Church is essentially 'en route,' on a journey, a pilgrimage.

A church which pitches its tents without looking out constantly for new horizons, which does not continually strike camp, is being untrue to its calling."[2]

Saying the Word . . . *Church*

The Church is to be a vital part of the life of every believer. The fellowship and rituals of the Church nourish us spiritually, and our active involvement in its ministries provides for us meaningful avenues of witness and service. Every follower of Jesus ought to be visibly identified with a local congregation and faithful in his or her participation in the life, work, witness, and support of that group.

Unfortunately, some people have become disillusioned or disappointed in the church and therefore fail to actively take their place among the "called-out ones." We must remember that Christ calls us not only "out from" but also to *gather together.* "Let us not give up meeting together, as some are in the habit of doing, but let us encourage one another—and all the more as you see the Day approaching" (Heb. 10:25).

How unfortunate it is if we let those human aspects and flaws that will be manifest from time to time within the Church dampen our enthusiasm or commitment to be part of the Body of Christ! Christ loved the Church and gave himself for it. His strong resolve was expressed when He declared, "On this rock I will build my church, and the gates of Hades will not overcome it" (Matt. 16:18).

We cannot be all that Christ calls us to be, nor do all that He asks of us, if we fail to be actively involved in the life of the Church.

Are you part of the life of a local congregation?

What is it about the Church that is most meaningful and helpful to you? How can you make it better?

Prayer

Holy One, bless Your Church around the world. With Paul we pray, "Unto [You] be glory in the church by Christ Jesus throughout all ages, world without end. Amen" [Eph. 3:21, KJV].

*No matter how
many
communes
anybody
invents, the
family always
creeps back.*

—Margaret Mead

Family

Parents and their children; any group of persons
closely related by blood, as parents, children, un-
cles, aunts, and cousins.

SEEING THE WORD . . . *FAMILY*

Each year from late summer into autumn, the skies in
the Midwest are filled with birds headed south for the winter. The "interstate flyways" traffic is bumper to bumper.
This annual migration is one of the great wonders of God's
creation, and it's a sure sign of fall.

Every year as summer turns the corner to autumn, I
find myself longing for a return trip as well, one that would
take me back to where I was raised. Perhaps it's because I
have so many fond memories of childhood during the fall.

I recall the early mornings on my way to elementary
school, walking past Brubaker's grain elevator. There in the

wide street would form a long line of red farm trucks, brimming with corn, waiting to make a deposit. What a sight for a small boy!

I would skip across the railroad tracks that separated the elevator from the Chevrolet dealership, stopping to press my nose against the glass to see the new cars. Then on to the schoolyard.

At the end of the day I would gather part of my belongings (I never could manage to find everything) and start retracing my steps home again. For a while I took trombone lessons, and carrying that long case home, I pretended there was a machine gun in it. I could always count on my share of imaginary battles as I cut through the alley behind the Elliotts' house.

Nearer to my house was the aroma from Timmer's Cannery, where ketchup and tomato juice were produced in the late summer and early fall. And later in the season came the smell of burning leaves from neighbors' backyard fires.

Arriving home, I would find my mother waiting there for me—she would give me a hug as if she hadn't seen me for a month. My mom was the "mushy" type.

At least once in the fall our family would make a weekend migration from our home in Ohio to Olive Hill, Kentucky, to see all the kinfolk, who hadn't changed, and all the leaves, which had. My father used to say, "If you have any doubts about making it to heaven, you ought to go to Kentucky, 'cause it would be a shame to miss 'em both."

Lately I've wondered if we as humans have a kind of homing instinct like the birds—that certain something that draws us back to where our lives began. If this longing for home isn't inborn, then it was surely instilled in me by a mom and dad who made our home the most comfortable "nest" one could imagine.

There was discipline, but it was overshadowed by love. There were chores, but they were balanced by touch football and trips to the Dairy Queen. What a privilege to have been raised in a godly home!

HEARING THE WORD . . . *FAMILY*

Strong families aren't perfect; they make their share of mistakes. But like the famous mechanical bunny of the television commercial, they just keep going and going and going.

In strong families, individual needs take a backseat to the needs of the family, and family members support one other through thick and thin. Whatever the type or situation, strong families survive by keeping their priorities straight. They are involved outside the home with neighbors, relatives, community activities, and churches.

Discipline of children, with both guidelines and limitations, is a key factor in strong families. There are clearly understood rules that are fairly enforced.

Parents teach children responsibility, right from wrong, and everyone knows what's expected.

The atmosphere is warm and trusting in strong families, though not always peaceful. Parents and children give one another love, understanding, and unconditional acceptance. There is a strong heart-and-soul connection, even when there's disagreement. Children in strong families receive the family blessing.

Contrary to myth, strong families are not happy all the time. They encounter the frustrations and major problems experienced by everyone else. The difference is that strong families have an ability to cope with the stresses and grow stronger in the process.

Stable families communicate openly and frequently, though not always pleasantly—sometimes they argue with great intensity. Members of strong families know they can talk about problems openly, and they do.

Members of strong families sacrifice for each other. They do things as a family. They understand and respect children. Parents in strong families invest their time and energy willingly.

Strong families value education and have faith in God.

Within these families, individuals treat one another with respect and take responsibility for their own mistakes. They are helpful to others in need. They know how to solve problems and forgive failures. Individual achievements and talents are encouraged and celebrated.

The members of strong, healthy families call or write their parents, brothers, and/or sisters every week or so. They gather to celebrate birthdays and holidays. Strong families nurture traditions and rituals. They have at least one common meal together a day, share a bedtime ritual, and tell lots of stories.

Parents in strong families have a wholesome attitude about life. This leadership gives these families a realistic but positive and hopeful perspective.

SAYING THE WORD . . . *FAMILY*

"Unless the LORD builds the house, they labor in vain who build it" (Ps. 127:1, NKJV).

Below is a set of characteristics of a strong, healthy family. During a family mealtime, read them and ask each family member to evaluate the list. The goal is to discover the strengths you already have and to prepare your family to get even stronger.

1. You catch each other doing things right. You look for the good instead of focusing on the bad.
2. You've learned how to argue without losing your temper.
3. You deal with each day's problems as they arise, rather than letting them build up.
4. You've made family a top priority on your schedule. When the schedule gets tough, family wins.
5. You make time for casual conversations. You talk about feelings, intentions, thoughts, experiences, and actions.
6. You spend lots of time doing things together as a family, and you help each other try new things.

7. You don't label your family members. You allow each person to grow and change.

8. You express your appreciation for each person in your family.

9. You've learned an effective way to resolve conflicts that works for you and your family.

10. You've learned when to be flexible and when to be firm.

11. You've developed a team spirit around the house. Helping out teaches everyone responsibility. It's a mark of maturity.

12. You have heart-to-heart, informal talks with each family member on a regular basis.

13. You pray with each family member on a regular basis.

14. You've found a healthy way of dealing with stress —prayer, music, exercise, relaxation, humor, worship, pets, and so on.

15. Your family is aware of the rules and expectations at home. Although the rules may be challenged, they are respected.

16. You have found ways to have fun together on a regular basis.

17. You eat at least one meal a day together.

18. Your family attends church regularly and is involved with the life of the church.

19. You've developed your own family traditions, including those of birthdays, Christmas, Thanksgiving, anniversaries, and other special days.

20. You've cried with a family member in the last few months, and you've laughed with a family member in the last few months.

21. You share your work life. You let your children see you at work and meet your coworkers.

22. You share successes as a family, talking about the good things that happen during the day.

23. You share inspirational stories of people who stand for the values you appreciate.
24. You honor your children's creations and have set aside an area of the house for displaying their creations, awards, and schedules.
25. Your family speaks openly about church, faith, and religious issues.
26. You have found ways to talk with your children about tough issues like drugs, sex, race, and death.
27. Every once in a while you do something crazy with your family.
28. When your family faces a crisis, you pull together and find a way to deal with it successfully.
29. You feel safe and secure within your home.
30. When you make promises, you keep them.

PRAYER

It was You, O Lord, who said, "It is not good that man should be alone." Family had, and still has, its source in You. What a good idea! How enriched we are by the lives of those with whom we live! For this gift we give thanks.

Bless Your family—all humanity, Your redeemed family—the Church, and my family as well. May our shared life bring honor and joy to You. In Jesus' name. Amen.

*Trust in the LORD
with all your
heart, and lean
not on your own
understanding;
in all your ways
acknowledge Him,
and He shall
direct your paths.*

—Prov. 3:5-6, NKJV

Trust

Reliance on the integrity and ability of another.
Confident expectation. Hope.

SEEING THE WORD . . . *TRUST*

Many years ago my wife, Jill, and I were spending the weekend with some friends. They graciously gave us their bedroom, the master bedroom of the house.

Deep into the night I awoke to find their two-year-old daughter snuggled up between us in bed. She was already asleep in her room when we arrived, but evidently she became restless in the night and slipped down the hall into her parents' bedroom and crawled, she thought, into bed with them.

I wasn't sure what to do. I hated to go back to sleep and let her wake up to find her parents missing from their bed, replaced by two strangers. Yet, I also dreaded waking her in the middle of night. Not knowing what to do, I did what most husbands would do: I reached over the little girl and woke up my wife.

"Jill, Stephanie is in bed with us," I whispered. Jill calmly sized up the situation, got up, and leaned over the bed to pick Stephanie up. As she lifted her, the little girl awoke. Jill firmly yet gently held her close and said quietly, "Stephanie, this is Jill. I'm going to put you back in your own bed." I held my breath until I heard the little girl sweetly say, "OK."

What trust! I thought. Two arms lift her, a loving voice promises to take her safely back to where she belongs, and her response is one of childlike faith: "OK"—which is to say, "I don't know what's happening, and I can't see in this darkness, but I trust you."

Frederick Buechner tells of a time in his life when his daughter was terribly ill and he was fearful and depressed. As he sat in a parked car along a quiet roadside, a car came, seemingly out of nowhere, down the highway with a license plate that bore on it "the one word out of all the words in the dictionary that I needed most to see exactly then. The word was TRUST."[1]

The owner of the car turned out to be a trust officer in a bank, who later happened to hear Buechner tell that story. The banker found where Buechner lived and took him the plate. It was a little battered and rusted around the edges, but for Buechner, "it is also as holy a relic as I have ever seen."[2]

Hearing the Word . . . *Trust*

"What time I am afraid, I will trust in thee" (Ps. 56:3, KJV). Trust brings confidence and dispels anxiety and fear.

Bill Hybels writes, "As I walked toward the plane for my first sky diving attempt, I patted the parachute of the fellow in front of me and asked, 'Do you think these will open the way they say they will?'

"He turned and shot back, 'In about five minutes, we're both going to find out, aren't we?'"[3]

The simple truth is this: the only way to find out for sure if a parachute is going to work is to jump out of a plane and pull the ripcord. You won't know for sure until you jump.

Trusting is not theory—it's action. It must be tried and tested. It's so easy to say we trust God and yet in reality put our confidence in our own wisdom and ways. The psalmist writes, "Some trust in chariots and some in horses, but we trust in the name of the LORD our God" (Ps. 20:7). How like many of us!

It's tough to trust, because we know so very little that's genuinely trustworthy. When I was a small boy, my older brother and I were playing in the yard one summer afternoon. We ran into the house where our mother was ironing. She offered to get us a cold drink and, as we waited for her to return, my brother said to me, "John, put your hand on the iron and see if it's hot." Without questioning him or thinking of any reason why I shouldn't do that, I placed the palm of my hand squarely on the hot iron.

I learned two important lessons that day—(1) not to touch a hot iron, and (2) not to trust my older brother!

It's not unusual for any of us to get "burned" occasionally when we put confidence in someone else. It's easy, therefore, for us to become tentative and a little less trusting than we might otherwise be. However, even though circumstances and individuals might disappoint us, God remains faithful and trustworthy.

SAYING THE WORD . . . *TRUST*

Have you proven God trustworthy in your life? God can be trusted in both the big and small things of life, but you'll never know that for sure until you jump. Has His trustworthiness failed you, or has it simply been untried?

The scriptures are clear: "Trust in the L<small>ORD</small> with all your heart, and lean not on your own understanding; in all your ways acknowledge Him, and He shall direct your paths" (Prov. 3:5-6, N<small>KJV</small>).

God can be trusted "in all your ways." This means God can be trusted to help you build a marriage, raise a family, or live without a mate. God can be trusted with your finances and with your vocation. He is trustworthy when you have to make decisions, when tragedy strikes, or when you're faced with a change in your life. *In all your ways—* what a promise!

Trust is faith in action, faith made visible, faith applied.

Can you identify an area in your life in which you need to let go and let God "direct your path"? What would you do, how would you respond, in that situation if you knew for sure God would not disappoint you? Don't hold back. Don't delay. Try it.

P<small>RAYER</small>

Dependable God, You alone are worthy of praise. I praise You. You alone are trustworthy. I trust You. May my hope be in You alone, not in wealth or health or human resources. May my confidence flow from Your faithfulness. May my future rest in the grip of Your grace.

I will trust though I cannot see. In the strong name of Jesus I pray. Amen.

> *Worship is the missing jewel of the evangelical church.*
>
> —A. W. Tozer

Worship

To honor and reverence. An act of expressing such honor and reverence.

SEEING THE WORD . . . *WORSHIP*

Have you ever wondered why people fight traffic, pay high prices for tickets, and sit for hours on hard seats just to watch a baseball game? Who needs to go to a crowded stadium full of screaming fans—especially when you can sit at home in your favorite chair, munch on something from your own kitchen, and watch the game on television?

The last time I went to a ball game was at Wrigley Field, home of the Chicago Cubs. Unknowingly I sat in a seat that had chewing gum on it and bore a rather tacky smear on my trousers for the rest of the day. Then a woman sitting behind me tried to step over the row of seats beside me, and as she did, she fell on me, pouring a cup of hot coffee all over my jacket. That wasn't all bad, though—it was the first time I had been warm all day.

Nevertheless, the enthusiasm generated by a nearly full stadium, skilled athletes, and big plays was contagious. I could have stayed home and been dry and clean and warm; but I would have missed something. A baseball game is more than just what happens on the field. It's what happens on the field magnified by all the fans in the stands. Being there meant that I was in fact part of the game. Attending was far more exciting than sitting in front of a television set.

"Being there" is an important element in worship as well as recreation. Some may feel that they can worship just fine sitting at home alone watching a religious television program, but *watching isn't worshiping.*

HEARING THE WORD . . . *WORSHIP*

When you consider all the various biblical words translated *worship,* you find that worship involves both *attitudes,* such as awe, reverence, and respect, and *actions,* such as bowing, praising, and serving. It's both a subjective experience and an objective activity. Worship is not an unexpressed feeling, nor is it empty formality. It must involve the whole person—mind, emotions, body, and will.

Evelyn Underhill has defined worship as "the total adoring response of man to the one Eternal God."

Worship is to intentionally practice the presence of God. It is opening oneself to experience the inner presence of God's grace and peace. It is counting one's blessings and giving thanks. To worship is to recenter oneself on God.

Whether in a cathedral or a cottage, worship inspires and realigns our lives through a clear vision of God. It brings a renewed recognition that this is God's world and that we are His children.

Although the Christian faith is individually appropriated and one can certainly experience wonderful moments of private worship, there is a corporate nature to worship that is to be nurtured and expressed. The discipline of weekly worship is an important means of grace. It is a strengthening habit for one's spiritual life.

The Bible calls on us to congregate: "Let us not give up meeting together, as some are in the habit of doing, but let us encourage one another—and all the more as you see the Day approaching" (Heb. 10:25).

There is a danger for any of us if we habitually miss attending church services and gatherings. If we fail to meet together for worship, we cut ourselves off from many of the blessings of God that come to us through the Church. And the verse from Hebrews suggests that meeting together enables us to encourage one another.

Corporate worship encourages us through the fellowship involved. When I was at Wrigley Field, the presence of the other fans drew me more fully into what was happening on the field and often lifted my level of interest and enthusiasm. As others cheered, I would take note and often cheer as well. I felt part of something bigger than myself.

We are encouraged by expressing the faith publicly through song and sacrament, through prayer and preaching. Worship takes on a richness when shared with others, and this experience stays with us as we leave. Throughout the week after the game, I remembered certain key plays and events from that outing. I enjoyed the experience repeatedly through reflection.

Shared experiences create social and spiritual bonds. My trip to the game was as part of a group who attended with me. Often when I'm in conversation with others who were there, we replay the events. We move in conversation to that common experience. When you pray with someone, hear the Word together, sing as part of the congregation, or even simply share a pew and shake a hand, there takes place a certain nurturing of relationship and the creation of spiritual memories and landmarks that can continue to nourish us for years to come.

But even more fundamental than the strong fellowship of worship is the private spiritual blessings that accompany genuine worship. As we worship, we're responding to God with adoration, praise, thanksgiving, proclamation, confession, and commitment.

Certainly forms of worship have changed and will continue to change, but the elements of worship and the avenues of worship—prayer, singing, giving, preaching, listening, and the sacraments—will transcend these changes. For worship is not merely our duty to God nor just something He requires and expects from His children. Worship refreshes and sustains the people of God. Worship is nourishment for our spirits. Without it we become weak and faint; through it we are strengthened and encouraged.

It used to be that the largest places in the world for public gatherings were the cathedrals. Now it's the sports arenas. That's a sad commentary on our social and spiritual priorities. However, it's still true that on any given Sunday there are many more people in worship than those who fill all the stadiums and recreational parks of the world. May it continue to be so as we renew our commitments to be in church and be part of the people of God assembled for His glory.

SAYING THE WORD . . . *WORSHIP*

"My heart says of you, 'Seek his face!' Your face, LORD, I will seek" (Ps. 27:8).

Worship is the acknowledgment of the "worth-ship" of God. It is at its essence the celebration of God and His mighty acts of grace. We extol Him, we sound His praises, we boast in Him. Genuine worship is to magnify God. It is the human response to the divine nature.

Jesus made it clear in His conversation with the woman of Samaria that there is both true and false worship (John 4:19-24). What passes for worship in some congregations may not be acceptable to God at all. The Pharisees thought they were practicing exemplary worship, but Jesus noted, "These people draw near to Me with their mouth, and honor Me with their lips, but their heart is far from Me. And in vain they worship Me, teaching as doctrines the commandments of men" (Matt. 15:8-9, NKJV).

You may or may not be pleased with all the aspects of

the worship services at your church. Nevertheless, you can worship meaningfully if your focus remains on God and not on your failed expectations.

What is the most meaningful part of worship for you?

What can *you* do to make worship more meaningful?

How do you prepare for worship? What more could you do before worship begins to make it more meaningful?

PRAYER

Father, thank You for Your patience with me!

When I think of how many worship services I have wasted, and how many worship services I have criticized, I feel very ashamed. Lead me in worship; prompt my mind and spirit in response to You. Fill me with wonder, and accept my praise and thanksgiving. In Jesus' name I pray. Amen.

> *The greatest
> discovery of my
> generation is
> that human
> beings can alter
> their lives by
> altering their
> attitudes of
> mind.*
>
> —William James

Attitude

Manner, disposition, feeling, position with regard to a person or thing.

SEEING THE WORD . . . *ATTITUDE*

After a brisk morning walk, an old fellow and his grandson sat for a time together on a bench at a gas station near the edge of town. As they watched folks come and go, a tall fellow, who had stopped for gas while passing through, struck up a conversation with them: "Tell me—what kind of a town is this?"

"What kind of town are you from?" replied the older gentleman.

The stranger said, "In the town I'm from, everyone is very critical of each other. The neighbors all gossip about everyone, and it's a very negative place in which to live."

The man on the bench replied, "You know, that's just how this town is."

A few minutes later a family, also passing through town, stopped for gas. The car slowly turned in and rolled to a stop at the pump nearest to the bench. The children bounded out of the car and darted inside. The gentleman driving began to pump the gas and as he stretched his legs a bit, he struck up a conversation with the fellow on the bench.

"Is this town a pretty good place to live?" he asked.

"What about the town you're from? How is it?"

"Well, in the town I'm from, everyone's very close and always willing to lend their neighbor a hand. There's always a hello and friendly handshake everywhere you go."

The older fellow replied, "You know, that's a lot like our town."

As this second car drove off, the youngster asked his grandfather, "Gramps, how come when that first man came into town you told him that this was a terrible place to live, and when this other fellow asked you, you told him it is a wonderful place to live?"

The grandfather looked down with a smile and gently responded, "No matter where you move, you take your own attitude with you—and that's what makes it a terrible or wonderful place."

HEARING THE WORD . . . ATTITUDE

There was once a man whose ax was missing, and he suspected that his neighbor's son had stolen it. The boy walked like a thief, looked like a thief, and spoke like a thief. Then one day the man found his ax under his own stack of wood. The next day he saw the neighbor's son—the boy walked, looked, and spoke like any other child.

This story illustrates the power of attitude to color perceptions. Our attitudes form the palette from which we paint our lives. If the shades are dark and dreary, all of life will take on that hue. But if the colors of our life are bright and balanced, then we can respond to each challenge and every person in positive ways.

Attitudes are shaped (and misshaped) over a lifetime. Changing attitudes is more than just changing our minds. Experience, understanding, maturity, and feelings all impact our attitudes.

We may often need to simply act appropriately, regardless of our present attitude. Feelings and attitudes often follow actions. To act friendly is a big part of becoming a friendly person. To submit to the disciplines of the faith will often deepen our commitment and attitude toward the things of God.

"Whether you think you can or think you can't—you are right" was the observation of Henry Ford.

SAYING THE WORD . . . *ATTITUDE*

Anne Frank learned the power of attitude under difficult circumstances. Forced along with her family into hiding from the Nazis during World War II, she kept a diary. In it she wrote,

> In the evening when I lie in bed and end my prayers with the words, "I thank you God, for all that is good and dear and beautiful," I am filled with joy. Then I think about "the good" of going into hiding, of my health and with my whole being of the "dearness" of Peter, of that which is still embryonic and impressionable and which we neither of us dare to name or touch, of that which will come sometime: love, the future, happiness and of "the beauty" which exists in the world. . . . I don't think then of all the misery, but of the beauty that still remains.[1]

Anne chose the focus of her life. Her attitude transformed her circumstances. The same can happen for anyone who will let the grace and hope of God enrich his or her attitudes. United States President Abraham Lincoln said, "Most people are as happy as they make up their minds to be."

You can alter your life by altering your attitude.

- Your attitude at the beginning of a difficult task is the most important factor in determining the success of the outcome. If you confidently believe you can succeed, even in the face of difficulty, you will be successful on most occasions.

- Your attitude toward others determines their attitude toward you. Look for the best in people, and treat them with respect.

- Before you can achieve the kind of life you want, you must think, act, talk, and conduct yourself in every way consistent with that desire. Hold a mental picture of the person you want to be.

- A great attitude is not the result of success. Success is the result of a great attitude. Since your mind can hold only one thought at a time, make each thought constructive and positive. Take control of the inner conversation, and don't let negative self-talk defeat you.

PRAYER

Teach me, O God, so to use all the circumstances of my life today that they may bring forth in me the fruits of holiness rather than the fruits of sin.

Let me use disappointments as material for patience.
Let me use success as material for thankfulness.
Let me use danger as material for courage.
Let me use reproach as material for longsuffering.
Let me use praise as material for humility.
Let me use pleasure as material for temperance.
Let me use pains as material for endurance.[2]

—John Baillie

> *Sloth kills*
> *the desire to*
> *change for*
> *the better.*
> —Tony Campolo

Sloth

Indolence. Idleness. Spiritual apathy and inactivity.

SEEING THE WORD . . . *SLOTH*

As a sophomore in high school, I was subjected to a "new approach" for learning geometry. It was a self-paced program in which each student was given a workbook designed to teach us everything we needed to know about Geometry I.

The good news was that we could take the entire semester to finish the workbook; each individual was free to work at his or her own pace. However, as the opposite side of a single coin, the *bad* news was that we could take the entire semester to finish the workbook; each individual was free to work at his or her own pace. We learned that this option could be either a curse or a blessing. It depended solely on the individual.

Tests were available whenever you felt you were ready. The teacher became a proctor and a passive resource person.

At first, this freedom to learn at a self-paced rate was a glorious freedom. In the beginning we worked hard because we didn't have to, but little by little this freedom and the lack of a set pace began to entrap many of us. We studied on the days we wanted to and didn't on the days we didn't. Soon the "didn't" days began to multiply.

Several of us fell well behind the pace, but initially it didn't seem to matter. The teacher didn't say anything, and no one else noticed.

Before we knew it, we were enslaved by this freedom. The workbook became a tyrant as we fell farther and farther behind.

At midsemester, the teacher talked with those of us who were not yet halfway through our work. He cautioned us about the mounting number of pages that were to be completed by the end of the term. Yet, he left our freedom intact. We could heed his word and buckle down to business, catch up with the others, and finish on time, or we could continue our geometric slide toward disaster.

I completed the work, but not without some long nights and added stress.

How easy it would have been to just do a little every day, to keep up with the work week by week! I squandered this chance to use the freedom given me—freedom that came from an opportunity to do more rather than an excuse to do less.

Why is it so hard to do that which in the long run is in our best interest? What is it about us that causes us to choose present ease over future benefit?

HEARING THE WORD . . . *SLOTH*

Sloth was the first among the seven deadly sins identified by the Church during the Middle Ages. The word is seldom used today, yet the reality is very much with us. In fact, the culture around us nurtures sloth.

Sloth causes us to put off until tomorrow what should be done today. Voltaire observed, "Sloth is a rust that attaches itself to the most brilliant metals." We are all susceptible to the corrosive influence of sloth. It manifests itself in many ways, including procrastination, lack of spiritual discipline, and general apathy.

- Sloth puts ease before duty and kills spiritual growth and nurture. Spiritual growth is hard work; the very word *disciple* flows from the same root as *discipline.*
- Sloth makes loving nearly impossible. For love requires commitment and work, and those who are slothful are seldom willing to expend the time and energy required of love. Marriages fail because husbands and wives are not willing to pay the price in effort and commitment to rekindle and nurture relationships. Sloth prevents parents from exercising consistent discipline—it's easier to give in.
- Sloth dissipates health through lack of exercise.
- Sloth kills the desire to change for the better.
- Sloth deadens the heart and soul.
- Sloth nurtures laziness and indolence.
- Sloth makes life a spectator sport to be watched from an easy chair or pew.
- Sloth nurtures a "room service" approach to life. It seeks to be served rather than looking for ways to serve.

Being slothful and being lazy are not the same, though they are first cousins. Everyone has a lazy day from time to time; in fact, we need moments when we're idle and reflective and restful. There's nothing wrong with being relaxed. An individual taking a nap, swinging in a hammock, or sitting on a swing watching the grass grow may at other times be very conscientious and productive.

The slothful person, on the other hand, may appear to be quite busy when in reality he or she is not positive or productive.

Saying the Word . . . *Sloth*

The answer to sloth lies beyond "turning over a new leaf." The remedy is the living presence of the Holy Spirit within. He manifests the fruit of the Spirit and provides the spiritual energy to shake off the chains of sloth.

Sloth deadens, but the Spirit gives life. Sloth thrives on self-centeredness; the Spirit recenters us in Christ.

• Take a moment just now to list the items in your life that need added attention. This might be as basic as cleaning out a closet or writing a thank-you note or as vital as repairing a relationship. What are the unfinished or unresolved issues and tasks of your life that bring anxiety as you think of them?

Commit these issues and items to God, and begin now, with the Lord's help to act—for action is the antidote to sloth.

PRAYER

O Thou who never sleeps nor slumbers, awaken within me a renewed energy and desire for spiritual growth. May I hunger and thirst after righteousness. I confess my inclination to put myself first, to care more for my ease than Your will. Forgive me, and through Your Holy Spirit empower me for service.

I commit myself to You. Breathe into me the strength and grace necessary to be a fully devoted follower. In Jesus' name. Amen.

> *Can the
> liberties of a
> nation be
> secure when we
> have removed
> a conviction
> that these
> liberties are the
> gift of God?*
>
> —Thomas Jefferson

Freedom

A setting at liberty. Release from bondage, imprisonment, or restraint. Ability to do something at will.

SEEING THE WORD . . . *FREEDOM*

She stands 350 feet tall, she weighs 205 tons, her nose is 4½ feet long, her mouth is a yard wide, her skin is green, and I love her very much. I refer, of course, to the Statue of Liberty, located in New York Harbor. Her official title is "Liberty Enlightens the World." She is well over 100 years old, and 2 million people stop to see her every year.

I first met her when I was a high school boy. My older brother and I had traveled alone from our small hometown in Ohio to New York City to visit one of his college friends. One evening we took a boat trip into the harbor to see the skyline and visit the lady with the lamp. The night was windy and cold. Most people stayed inside the little cabin area—but I walked to the front of the boat, stood there in the night air, and looked out upon a world I had never seen before.

As we came near the statue, it seemed for just a moment that she was alive and that there were just the two of us—I looking up at her and she looking out at the world.

The Statue of Liberty is not placed to be seen well from every angle. If you look at her from the back, she's rather stiff and awkward. If you look at her from the island on which she stands, she's so overwhelming that you can't really see her well. If you go to Manhattan or New Jersey, she's too far away to be accurately observed.

The way to see her best is from the water just as you enter New York Harbor. There's a certain place, just after passing the narrows, where the line and contour of her body and the flow of her gown sweep up to her torch so that she looks as though she's about to step forward from her pedestal.

The sponsors of this massive project encouraged writers of the day to give manuscripts to be auctioned. The proceeds would be used for the pedestal and the erection of the statue. American poet Emma Lazarus was asked to write a poem to aid in this effort. Her poem was called "The New Colossus." She had never seen the statue, for it was still in pieces in a wooden shed waiting to be assembled, but she was able to capture its meaning as she wrote, "Give me your tired, your poor, / Your huddled masses yearning to breathe free."

Hearing the Word . . . *Freedom*

In her book *Killers of the Dream,* Lillian Smith writes, "Freedom and responsibility are Siamese twins—they die if they are parted."

The Statue of Liberty stands as a great symbol of liberty and justice. Her presence is perhaps more important today than ever before. Our world is changing. In some places liberty and justice are flourishing after long periods of oppression and dormancy. In other places tyranny triumphs. Part of the problem is that liberty and justice are too often seen as roadblocks to political power and ambition.

The lady depicted in the Statue of Liberty holds a great stone tablet. It is not there by accident. Frédéric-Auguste Bartholdi, who designed the statue, wanted the viewer to be reminded of Moses coming down from Mount Sinai with the stone tablets of the Law of God. The implied message is that liberty and justice rest on the God's Word.

The New Testament message of Jesus' saving grace reminds us that liberty and justice find their source and fulfillment in God and His love for all people. "The Spirit of the Lord is on me, because he has anointed me to preach good news to the poor. He has sent me to proclaim freedom for the prisoners and recovery of sight for the blind, to release the oppressed, to proclaim the year of the Lord's favor" (Luke 4:18-19).

Our love for God compels us to work for freedom and justice for all. The Church must be a strong and steady voice worldwide, reminding people everywhere that liberty and justice are more than political concepts—they are Kingdom values. The Old Testament call is to "proclaim liberty throughout the land to all its inhabitants" (Lev. 25:10) and to "let justice roll on like a river" (Amos 5:24).

SAYING THE WORD . . . *FREEDOM*

Not long ago a public school teacher distributed to his fourth grade class a parchmentlike copy of the Declaration of Independence. Each student was to look at this copy and pass it on to the next member of the class. As it made its rounds, it came to the desk of a little boy, a first-generation American. He looked at it most reverently, and then, before passing it on to the next student, he bravely took his pen and signed his own name.

We, too, must take personal ownership of these values. Liberty means responsibility.

Commit yourself to civic responsibility, including voting and supporting candidates who uphold Christian values.

Recognize that all around us are individuals who live in bondage. This takes many forms, including the bondage of guilt, addiction, and emotional scarring.

Would you ask God to enable you "to proclaim freedom for the prisoners and recovery of sight for the blind, to release the oppressed" (Luke 4:18), knowing that those whom Christ sets free are free indeed?

PRAYER

O God of liberty, set me free from all those things that keep be from being a fully devoted follower. Enable me to be an ambassador and agent of freedom to all who are imprisoned in body, mind, or spirit. In Jesus' name I pray. Amen.

*To waste
your time
is to waste
your life.*

Time

A measurable continuum in which events occur
in succession from past to present to future.

SEEING THE WORD . . . *TIME*

You just can't believe it. You've never won anything before in your entire life. You barely remember filling out the
registration card a few weeks ago as you left the grocery
store. But the manager is on the phone telling you the good
news—you've won!

Yes, you've been selected to participate in the "Fifteen
Minutes of Madness" special promotion. You will be given
15 minutes to race up and down the aisles of the store and
fill your shopping cart with as much food as you can.

In fact, you may fill as many carts as you want until
your time runs out, and everything in those carts will be
yours—absolutely free.

It's a once-in-a-lifetime opportunity.

The day arrives, the store is filled with spectators, the
shelves are stocked, and the aisles are clear. Your only limi-
tation is time. Suddenly the whistle sounds.

You begin racing through the aisles. The crowd cheers
you on. Suddenly, however, the thrill is gone. Your palms

begin to sweat, your breath is short, and you tighten your grip on the handle of the cart.

Your vision blurs as you realize that there are so many aisles, so many choices, and so little time. You suddenly see how unprepared you are for such an adventure.

If only you had made a list of the things you needed most. If you had an aisle chart so that you could easily find what you wanted rather than running aimlessly, grabbing only what you happen to see.

You could have done so many things to maximize this opportunity. But you didn't think it through, and the time is passing. Suddenly the whistle sounds again.

"No!" you say to yourself. "It can't be over. I've just started." As you wheel your cart to the front, you see that all you have accumulated is 17 bags of pork rinds, a case of miniature marshmallows, three pounds of kitty litter, and a cantaloupe.

You've wasted this once-in-a-lifetime opportunity.

HEARING THE WORD . . . *TIME*

We are often like that frustrated shopper as we face life. The shelves are lined from floor to ceiling with a multitude of beautiful opportunities begging for our time. Daily our vision is blurred by the sheer volume of worthwhile activities available to us. Each is wrapped in brightly colored packages just waiting to be claimed.

We have an infinite number of opportunities but a finite amount of time, and the clock is running continually. Every moment is a moment we will never have again.

Tom Craik, a high school counselor, observed:

> I'm thirty-one years old next month. When I divide that by two, I'm fifteen and a half. Believe it or not, that was just yesterday. Double it, and I'm sixty-two. Believe it or not, I think that's tomorrow. Sometime yesterday morning my son was born. Today he's almost a year old. Tomorrow he'll be fifteen. Where

does it all go? What's happened to the "dreams"? And you know something else? I know less today than I did yesterday and probably more than I will know tomorrow. Zoom! There it goes. There I go![1]

There ought to be a godly sense of urgency about life. The time we have is a sacred trust from God. Time is life itself. To waste your time is to waste your life. To invest your time unwisely is to invest your life unwisely.

The Christian's stewardship of time begins with a recognition that time, as all of life, belongs to God. What we call "our time" is not really ours, but God's. It's a gift He has given us to manage, to use for His glory.

One of the intriguing things about this call to manage our time well is that we all have the same amount of time in the course of a day. The most productive person among us has no more time than the person who lets days pass without any eternal benefit accruing.

Time cannot be accumulated like money or stockpiled like raw materials. It cannot be turned on and off. It cannot be replaced once it is gone. It is irretrievable. We are forced to spend it, whether we choose to or not, at a fixed rate of 60 seconds per minute, 60 minutes per hour.

There really is no such thing as "saving" time, for we have to spend it. But we can determine, at least in part, *how* we will spend it.

"Therefore be careful how you walk, not as unwise men, but as wise, making the most of your time, because the days are evil. So then do not be foolish, but understand what the will of the Lord is" (Eph. 5:15-17, NASB).

Saying the Word . . . *Time*

Do you feel you have enough time for the really important things in your life?

Our goal is not to find more time (for we have all the time there is), but to use our time more wisely: *making the most of your time.* That phrase is translated in the King

James Version as "redeeming the time." There's a sense in which we give something in exchange for our time, and whatever we give bestows value upon that time. Time used for God has great value.

Keep a time log for a week, noting how each 15-minute period was used. Once you complete that revealing assignment, ask yourself if you're pleased with your use of time. The answer will probably leap from the page. Take time to plan each day carefully in light of your primary values.

Some years ago a fellow named Ivy Lee was hired by the president of Bethlehem Steel Corporation as a management consultant. The president challenged Lee, "Show me a way to get more things done with my time, and I'll pay you anything within reason."

Lee studied the company and the president's work habits for a period of time and then handed the president a sheet of paper with this plan:

> Write down the most important tasks you have to do tomorrow. Number them in order of importance. When you arrive in the morning, begin at once on No. 1 and stay on it until it is completed. Recheck your priorities; then begin with No. 2 . . . then No. 3. . . . Make this a habit every working day. Pass it on to those under you. Try it as long as you like; then send me your check for what you think it is worth.

The idea helped turn Bethlehem Steel into the biggest independent steel producer of its day.[2]

Remember: time is your life! Give your life to the things that are most important.

PRAYER

Maker and keeper of time itself, thank You for this wonderful gift. Teach me to measure my days with eternity in mind. Forgive me for wasted hours and squandered opportunities. I commit myself to "redeeming the time" You give me. In Jesus' name I pray. Amen.

*Winter is on
my head,
but spring is
in my heart.*

—Victor Hugo

Age

An individual's development as measured
in terms of the passing of time; an advanced
stage of life; to become old.

SEEING THE WORD . . . *AGE*

"Ninety-five," he thought as he stood before them,
waiting for the applause to subside. "It sounds old. I must
seem very old to most of them out there. But strangely
enough, I don't feel old at all. It's just another birthday like
all the others . . . another year behind me . . . and the best
of life is still ahead." These were the thoughts of Sir William
Mulock, Chief Justice of Ontario, as he prepared to address
a group of friends, family, and colleagues who had gathered
to mark this milestone in his life.

His voice was firm and clear as he spoke. It was the
voice of a man who loved life, who embraced his work with
vigor and his neighbor with grace. He began by saying:

I am still at work, with my hand to the plow, and
my face to the future. The shadows of evening lengthen
about me, but morning is in my heart. I have lived
from the forties of one century to the thirties of the

next. I have had varied fields of labor, and fill contact with men and things, and have warmed both hands before the fire of life.

The testimony I bear is this: that the Castle of Enchantment is not yet behind me. It is before me still, and daily I catch glimpses of its battlements and towers. The rich spoils of memory are mine. Mine, too, are the precious things of today—books, flowers, pictures, nature, and sport. The first of May is still an enchanted day to me. The best thing of all is friends. The best of life is always further on. Its real lure is hidden from our eyes, somewhere behind the hills of time.

The simple eloquence of Mulock's words, his serene contentment at the age of 95, touched the heart of every listener. Men of 50, 60 felt the weight of the years slip from their solders. "Every man over forty should carry a copy of Sir William's speech in his pocket," declared one newspaper in discussing the event editorially.

Sir William Mulock died in 1944 at the age of 100. He enjoyed a rich and rewarding life to the very end. Though his voice was stilled over half a century ago, the message he gave on his 95th birthday lingers: "The best of life is always further on."

I attended a Rotary Club meeting a few years ago and was introduced to a fellow in his 60s who was in the insurance business. After talking with me for a few moments, he in turn introduced me to the gentleman seated on the other side of him. It was his father, a spry gentleman in his early 90s. I greeted him and was surprised to learn that he, too, was still in the insurance business. Noting my surprise, his son said with some seriousness, "I keep wanting to retire, but my dad won't let me!"

HEARING THE WORD . . . *AGE*

The Bible assures us that old age is a virtue and a blessing. However, in the youth-oriented culture of today, that emphasis is often lost. So there are different ways of viewing age: "You are old and worn out and thus useless" or "You are wise and experienced, thus indispensable."

Which do you choose to believe? Certainly each stage of life has its strengths and weaknesses. If life is to be measured only by physical vitality, then as you grow older, you become less valued. But age has its inherent strengths as well as its obvious drawbacks.

In the introduction to his book *The Longing for Home,* Frederick Buechner writes:

> When I was young . . . I lived as though my time was endless. When I was in my fifties and early sixties even, I deluded myself with the fantasy that I was still somehow middle-aged and had roughly as much time left to live as I had lived already, which seemed endless enough for all practical purposes. But now that I find myself pushing seventy hard, I have finally begun to wise up. It is no longer just in my mind that I know I am rather a good deal closer to the end of my time than I am to its beginning. I know it in my stomach, and there is a lot of sadness in knowing. But that is by no means all there is. Who would want it to be day forever and never night, after all? Who would choose to be awake forever and never get a chance to sleep?[1]

Growing old is like living in a house that's in increasing need of repairs. The plumbing doesn't work right anymore. There are bats in the attic. Cracked and dusty, the windows are increasingly hard to see through. Yet while those things might be happening to the house, the one living within may still be youthful in spirit, attitude, and passion for life.

In Ps. 90 Moses offers a prayer to the Lord in which he asks, "Teach us to number our days aright, that we may gain a heart of wisdom" (v. 12). This is a petition for God's help to recognize the value of each day. Time is life, and it passes all too quickly.

We can live with confidence, even in the midst of the passing years, knowing that "all the days ordained for me were written in your book before one of them came to be" (Ps. 139:16).

Nobody grows old by merely living a number of years; people grow old by deserting their ideals and dreams. Years wrinkle the skin, but only a loss of enthusiasm wrinkles the soul.

"You are as young as your faith, as old as your doubt," wrote Samuel Ullman. "As young as your self-confidence, as old as your fear; as young as your hope, as old as your despair."

Robert Browning's magnificent poem "Rabbi ben Ezra" was published in 1864. It was widely quoted and discussed and remains so yet today. There are 32 stanzas to "Rabbi ben Ezra," but the first stanza is the best-known and most frequently quoted. The promise of these famous lines took a strong hold on the public; and they are today familiar to millions of people who have never read the poem in its entirety or even heard its name. It reads as follows:

Grow old along with me!
The best is yet to be,
The last of life, for which the first was made:
Our times are in His hand
Who saith, "A whole I planned,
Youth shows but half; trust God; see all, nor be afraid!"

Saying the Word . . . Age

The list varies depending upon which version you happen to come across. Yet each begins the same way: "You know you're getting older when . . ." This is followed by a series of characteristics associated with aging.

You know you're getting older when

- the gleam in your eyes is from the sun hitting your bifocals
- your knees buckle but your belt won't
- your children begin to look middle-aged

- your favorite part of the newspaper is "Twenty Years Ago Today"
- you have too much room in the house and not enough room in the medicine cabinet
- your broad mind and narrow waist have exchanged places
- your mind makes contracts that your body can't keep
- you feel like the morning after, but you haven't been anywhere

Aging does bring changes, and the best way to greet those changes is with a smile. We should view the aging process as a challenge but not as a threat. All of life is sacred, and each new day is a gift from God to be invested in things eternal.

"If wrinkles must be written upon our brows, let them not be written upon the heart," James Garfield wrote. "The spirit should not grow old."

Make a list of the things you would still like to do in life. Start today.

Be sure to truly celebrate your birthday.

Remember these words from Malcolm Forbes: "As you get older don't slow down, speed up. There's less time left."

PRAYER

O God of time and eternity, every day is a gift of grace and possibility. Help me to treasure each one so that I may not just grow old but also grow new. Let each day be a day of beginning. In Jesus' name. Amen.

> *Opportunities are usually disguised by hard work, so most people don't recognize them.*
>
> —Ann Landers

Work

Exertion or effort directed to produce or accomplish something; labor; toil.

Seeing the Word . . . Work

A nobleman who enjoyed the aesthetics of life hired a farmer to stand inside his castle and move back and forth with a hand pick, just as he would do in the field. The nobleman took great delight in the simple elegance of the farmer's sway, and he paid the farmer well for his "work." Still, after entertaining the nobleman for several days, the farmer refused to continue. "But I pay you generously," said the surprised nobleman, "many times more than you would make by working in the field. And you don't have to exert yourself nearly as much."

"You don't seem to understand," the farmer replied. "I cannot continue doing something—even if it takes no toil and effort—that doesn't produce. I would rather work much harder and be productive than be paid well to do something that bears no fruit."

Most people will work 160,000 hours during their lifetime. These hours can either be drudgery or a delight, depending upon their understanding of work.

HEARING THE WORD . . . *WORK*

Work is not something we do merely to make enough money to surround ourselves with material comforts. Work is a search for enduring meaning as well as for daily bread, for recognition as well as for pay, for service to others as well as for one's self-worth and pride. Prolonged leisure may seem attractive, but it's work that bestows satisfaction.

The biblical view is that work is part of God's plan for men and women. The psalmist praises God for the fact that "Man goes forth to his work" (Ps. 104:23, NASB). Paul writes, "If anyone will not work, neither let him eat" (2 Thess. 3:10, NASB).

The Old Testament teaches that work is to be regarded as a necessary, worthy, and God-appointed function of human life. The basic assumption of the biblical viewpoint is that work is a divine ordinance for the life of humanity. The fact that the fourth commandment is a command to rest from labor rests upon the biblical idea that people are workers by nature. The biblical writers recognize the dignity of work and indicate that it is expected that we should work.

Work is not to be understood as a result of the Fall or a punishment from God. Before the Fall, humanity was created to "fill the earth and subdue it. Rule over the fish of the sea and the birds of the air and over every living creature that moves on the ground" (Gen. 1:28). Certainly work, like all of life, was affected by the Fall, but it remains throughout Scripture as part of God's plan and purpose for humanity.

As a means of witnessing and expressing our faith, the New Testament calls upon believers to be honest and faithful in their work: "Whatever you do, work at it with all your heart, as working for the Lord, not for men" (Col. 3:23). This calls the people of God to affirm that Jesus is the Lord of their vocational lives and offer the quality of their work to the Lord as an expression of their devotion and stewardship.

Christian workers are to be dutiful and obedient and must render godly respect and honor to their employers. By their faithful and honest service, they commend the truth of Christian doctrine. Their work, though ostensibly performed for the benefit of earthly masters, is in truth the service of Christ himself. It must therefore be well and diligently done, whether it meets with earthly reward or not. It is the fulfillment of a duty, and its aim is not reward or profit, but the glory of Christ.

Elton Trueblood writes that we make a serious mistake if we think that work is not Christian unless it is work for the church: "Actually the witness made in regular employment may be far more significant and productive than any service rendered in free time."[1]

Work is not to be considered a curse, but a calling, a way to construct a better world in union with Christ. Work has meaning beyond itself, and this is recognized as one sees work as a divine mandate and as ministry.

Work is part of what it means to be human, and it is through the sanctifying of their work that people find its true dignity and meaning. The value of work lies beyond the particular nature of the work being done. Its value lies in sharing in God's purposes as expressed through work. It's an occasion for people to cooperate with God and share in His creative work.

The temptation for many believers is to center their lives on the activities and programs of the local church rather than seeing their mission to be in the world for the glory of God. Christians must see that it is in the daily labors of their working life that they, "the people of God," are in the center of the arena where the Church needs to be.

SAYING THE WORD . . . *WORK*

A young fellow rushed into a gas station and asked to use the telephone. The manager could not help overhearing the conversation, which began with the question, "Sir, could you use a hard-working, honest young man to work for you? [Pause] Oh . . . you already have a hardworking, honest young man? Well, thanks anyway."

The fellow hung up the phone with a smile. As he waked away, he began to whistle a cheerful tune.

"How can you be so cheery?" asked the eavesdropping service station manager. "I thought the man you were talking to already had someone and couldn't hire you."

The young fellow answered, "Well, you see—I'm the hardworking, honest young man. I was just checking up on my job!"[2]

Too many people are ready to carry the stool when the piano needs to be moved.

Robert Slocum gives five guidelines for helping integrate faith and vocational work.[3] The first guideline is to note that "Because work originated with God, it follows that we are to look at work as something to which God calls us and as something he can use to give divine order to our lives."[4]

How we work; the quality of our work is also a Christian concern. Poor work becomes a disservice to God and the world around us.

A second principle identified by Slocum concerns the Christian's motivation for work. It's not the material benefits but the witness and ministry provided through the avenue of work. "My motivation for daily work must be a desire to serve God as a steward of the earth and a steward of my own talents and aptitudes."[5]

Next, the issue of career goals and the future in relationship to vocation is addressed by the following guideline: "I must accept the fact that my unfolding future in my daily work is in God's hands."[6] This probes the issue of whether a person is willing to set aside personal or corporate goals to understand God's plans and purposes.

The fourth guideline speaks to the need for a strong sense of stewardship to pervade our understanding of the role of work in God's plans for us: "Even if the future is in God's hands, I have in my own hands the stewardship responsibility for developing my own talents, aptitudes, and abilities. This fourth guideline means that God can guide and direct my work life as I work at being a good steward of my personal resources."[7]

The individual question is "How can I develop and invest my aptitudes and skills as an act of responsible obedience to Jesus Christ?"

The final guideline has to do with our expectations of success and rewards. Simply stated, it's this: "It is up to God whether and how I am blessed."[8] We cannot measure vocational success on the standards of this world alone. Our work and the results of our work must constantly be yielded to God.

Along with these ways of seeing the integration of faith and vocational work, it can be said that work is also an occasion for service to others. The people of the work setting are part of the context of ministry. Working to the glory of God is not just an issue of being diligent on the job but also includes being loving and redemptive in relationship to those with whom and for whom we work.

Evangelism is often a by-product of clear witness and consistent living. The witness and call for response heralded in worship must be reinforced in the world at large. "Life proves itself Christian in the happenings of one's working life."[9]

A strong part of a Christian's commitment to serve God is seen in his or her integration of faith and vocational work. The Christian life and witness are severely hampered without this integration. "God cannot be loved in opposition to our daily working life, nor apart from it, but only served in it. In their work laity use their talents, show their virtues, and prove their fidelity."[10]

So faith makes a difference in how we view work and how we work. Bringing the gospel to all of life can flood our working hours with new meaning and potential. The hours spent at work can become "Kingdom hours" that provide a powerful witness to the world of the grace and glory of God. It is vital to the Church, the individual, and the world at large that such an integration take place in the life of every believer.

PRAYER

My God, Father and Savior, since you have commanded us to work in order to meet our needs, sanctify our labor that it may bring nourishment to our souls as well as to our bodies. Make us constantly aware that our efforts are worthless unless guided by your light and strengthened by your hand. Amen.

—John Calvin

*Father, I beg of
Thee a little
task to dignify
my days; 'tis all
I ask.*

—Edna St. Vincent Millay

*Love has no
meaning if it
isn't shared.*

—Mother Teresa

Charity

Generosity and helpfulness toward the needy.

SEEING THE WORD . . . *CHARITY*

Teresa was born August 26, 1910, into the home of a peasant family in Albania. Her family was poor, but they were devout, and she was taken regularly to church. As a teenager she felt a calling to a full-time religious vocation. At age 18 she entered a convent to prepare for a life of service as a Catholic sister.

She trained to be a teacher. One day a missionary spoke to her home parish about the great need for Christian workers in India. Teresa volunteered and was accepted for a teaching post in Calcutta.

She was well cared for at the convent. She had a simple but lovely room with beautiful gardens and did her teaching in a well-equipped school. However, not long after arriving in India, she made a trip to the dirtiest and poorest part of town. As she walked the streets alone, she encountered something she had never seen before: people dying, literally dying, in alleyways and side streets—and no one seemed to pay any attention to them.

She inquired and discovered that this was a common occurrence. "You'll get used to it," she was told. But it haunted her. She felt that Jesus Christ was saying to her, "I'm going to call you to serve the poorest of the poor. I'm calling you to minister, not to the living, but to the dying."

Teresa asked to be released from her position. It took two years, but finally she was given permission to live outside the school and serve those who were in such great need. With only a few dollars in her pockets, she went forth with no promise of a meal, shelter, or clothing. She was on her own and prayed, *Jesus, lead me to somebody who is dying all alone.*

Just two blocks away she came upon an old lady near death, lying in the gutter on the main street. Teresa picked her up and carried her to the nearest hospital. She was refused admittance. "But this woman is dying," Teresa explained.

"People die on the streets of Calcutta all the time," she was told. "We can't take her." But Teresa refused to leave until the hospital made room for her patient. She said, "If there is a God in heaven and a Christ we love, nobody should die alone."

Shortly thereafter, Teresa went to the city government and asked for an empty room—"a place where I can care for the dying." She was given an abandoned Hindu temple. Without money or medicine or backing or recognition, she began to gather up the dying and bring them to this place where they would receive at least a compassionate touch and a tender voice saying, "We love you—may you die in peace."[1]

Today, of course, Mother Teresa is remembered worldwide as a saint of God and an angel of mercy. Before her death in 1997, she was caring for over 10,000 in Calcutta and had established her own religious order called Missionaries of Charity, which serves in many countries. The only thing the sisters of this order own is a cotton garment and a pair of sandals.

HEARING THE WORD . . . *CHARITY*

"When you reap the harvest of your land, you shall not wholly reap the corners of your field, nor shall you gather the gleanings of your harvest. And you shall not glean your vineyard, nor shall you gather every grape of your vineyard; you shall leave them for the poor and the stranger" (Lev. 19:9-10, NKJV).

Love is the greatest of all virtues, and charity is love in action. This kind of love is the defining virtue of the Christian faith. Christian love is far more than emotion—it is a response of the whole person—the heart, mind, will, and body. Christian love is by definition active rather than passive.

In its highest expression, charity is a "hands-on," person-to-person enterprise. By its very definition, charity must involve the heart as well as the pocketbook. Too often folks practice telescopic charity—giving from a distance. For many that form of "charity" is not love in action but guilt at work. It expresses an "I'll give, but I don't want to get involved" attitude and spirit.

Charity asks, "What does this person need?" rather than "What does this person deserve?" Charity, therefore, must be practiced with no consideration of the recipient's worthiness. We must resist the inclination to render a judgment concerning the person in need: "It's his own fault" or "If she had been more responsible, she wouldn't be in this situation."

Love dare not be tied to a preposition—I'll love you "if" or "because." The love of God is unconditional, and thus Christian charity says, "I will show forth the love of God regardless of the 'why' behind the need."

SAYING THE WORD . . . *CHARITY*

Each day you are confronted with opportunities to help others, to forgive them, to have compassion for them, to be tolerant of them. Do you seize these opportunities, or do you let them slip away?

These everyday decisions not only have a direct impact on the people around you but also affect your spiritual life, for we are the ones nurtured by our acts of charity. God's love enriches our lives as we lovingly respond to others. Each time you choose (and it is a choice) to help someone, your soul grows and flourishes.

Jesus said, "As I have loved you, so you must love one another" (John 13:34). He also said, "Whatever you did for one of the least of these brothers of mine, you did for me" (Matt. 25:40). "I was hungry and you gave me something to eat. . . . I needed clothes and you clothed me" (vv. 35-36).

Once we love God deeply, we will love our neighbor to the same extent, because as we grow in our love for God, we begin to love the things God loves and care about the things God cares about. We begin to care more for others than for ourselves. This is love, not that we first loved God, but that He first loved us.

Mother Teresa observed, "The greatest disease in the West today is not TB or leprosy; it is being unwanted, unloved and uncared for. We can cure physical diseases with medicine, but the only cure for loneliness, despair, and hopelessness is love. There are many in the world who are dying for a little love. The poverty in the West is a different kind of poverty—it is not only a poverty of loneliness but also of spirituality. There's a hunger for love, as there is a hunger for God."[2]

Just as plants need the carbon dioxide that humans exhale, humans need the oxygen plants produce. Charity is yet one more expression of this pattern: the giver and the receiver need one another. More than the rich man does for the pauper, the pauper does for the rich man.

We are living in a time and culture that are more materially prosperous and yet more spiritually impoverished than ever before. Living a life of charity breaks this cycle of self-interest.

In what specific ways do you demonstrate this Christian grace of charity? Can you think of someone within your circle of acquaintance and influence who is in need physically, emotionally, financially, or spiritually? What response would God want you to make in light of that person's needs?

Remember: "Now abideth faith, hope, charity, these three; but the greatest of these is charity" (1 Cor. 13:13, KJV).

PRAYER

O generous God, giver of every good and perfect gift, kindle within me the flames of charity. Help me to miss neither my neighbor's nor my enemy's need. Loosen my grip on the things of this world so that with one hand I might take the hand of someone in need and with my other hold on to You.

Release me from being possessed by riches I do not need and grievances that weary me and mar Your presence in my life. You call me to share my very self with those in need. May I become a missionary of charity. In Jesus' name I pray. Amen.

*Am I not
destroying
my enemies
when I make
friends of
them?*

—Abraham Lincoln

Reconciliation

Bringing into agreement or harmony; becoming peaceable or friendly again.

SEEING THE WORD . . . *RECONCILIATION*

In the book *The Great Hunger* the principal character is a man named Peer Holm. Living beside Peer and his family was a man who had a vicious dog. Peer feared for the safety of his little girl, so he asked his neighbor, "Could you chain up your dog?" But the man refused.

One day the event Peer feared the most became a reality. As he came in from the field, he heard the screams of his little girl. He ran to her and tore the dog away, but it was too late. The life was gone from her body.

The sheriff shot the dog, and instead of running the man out of town, the townspeople simply shunned him. They would not speak to him or trade with him. In the spring when he plowed his field, no one would sell him seed. So his land was left barren.

Finally, one moonlit night, Peer Holm could take it no longer. He got up, took several bushels of his own seed, went next door, and worked through the night to sow the grain in the field of his neighbor.

Later in the spring, the villagers saw a bare spot in Peer Holm's field and grain growing in the field of his neighbor. They came to Holm and said, "You—you of all people. Why did you do it?"

He replied, "I did it in order that God might exist again in our community."[1]

HEARING THE WORD . . . *RECONCILIATION*

Golda Meir observed, "You cannot shake hands with a clenched fist."

Unresolved conflict is one of life's most destructive and harmful forces. Not only are relationships damaged, but a great deal of emotional time and energy is expended in nurturing the hurt, rehearsing the wrong, and anchoring ourselves to the past. Resentment becomes a straightjacket that imprisons us emotionally and spiritually. Only through reconciliation can the relationships be restored and we be set free.

Yet how often do we hold on to a broken relationship because we're convinced that we're the wronged party? We convince ourselves that if there is to be reconciliation, it must be initiated by the other person. After all, it is his or her fault. But the story of Peer Holm illustrates two great principles: *First,* it is often the one who has been wronged who must initiate and facilitate reconciliation. *Second,* there is an unmistakable tie between our relationship with others and our relationship with God.

These twin principles are seen clearly in God's reconciling grace extended to all who will accept it. The New Testament uses the term *reconcile* to refer both to the reconciliation of God with humanity and the reconciliation of individuals to each other. Paul writes:

> Therefore, if anyone is in Christ, he is a new creation; the old has gone, the new has come! All this is from God, who reconciled us to himself through Christ and gave us the ministry of reconciliation: that God was reconciling the world to himself in Christ, not counting men's sins against them. And he has committed unto us the message of reconciliation. We are therefore Christ's ambassadors, as though God were making his appeal through us. We implore you on Christ's behalf: Be reconciled to God *(2 Cor. 5:17-20)*.

It is God, the One who was wronged, "who reconciled us to himself." It was God who made the first move. It was God who, through His grace, was willing to forgive and forget. Although the sin of humankind brought estrangement, God remained faithful. It is God, a God of reconciliation, who calls us to himself.

His instrument of reconciliation is the Cross. It was through the death and resurrection of Jesus that the peace of reconciliation was established. Christ became the high priest, the "pontiff" or "bridge builder." His sacrifice alone spans the chasm of estrangement. He is "the Prince of Peace."

The heart of reconciliation rests with our reconciliation to God but is manifested in our reconciliation with others. "All this comes from the God who settled the relationship between us and him, and then called us to settle our relationships with each other" (2 Cor. 5:18, TM).

The verb form of *reconciliation* is *reconcile,* which means "to change." When applied to relationships, it means to change enmity into friendship, bringing together people who have been estranged.

SAYING THE WORD . . . *RECONCILIATION*

Parents refereeing children, neighbors at odds, coworkers straining to get along, friendships broken by misunderstanding, spiritual growth stunted by sin or lack of faith—all of these are occasions to speak the word *reconciliation* into your daily life.

Is the twofold nature of reconciliation at work in your life?

1. Have you been fully reconciled to God?
2. Is there an individual with whom you should seek reconciliation?
3. In what specific ways can you say the word *reconciliation* in your life this week? Will you?

"For God was pleased to have all his fullness dwell in [Christ], and through him to reconcile to himself all things, whether things on earth or things in heaven, by making peace through his blood, shed on the cross" (Col. 1:19-20).

PRAYER

O God of reconciliation, You do not hold a grudge, You keep no record of wrongs. O Peacemaker, search me just now. Is there anything within my life that fosters estrangement, anything that casts a shadow on our relationship? If so, reveal it to me that I might surrender it and be fully reconciled.

O Prince of Peace, help me to be an ambassador of reconciliation. Let me be quick to forgive and eager to exchange my hurt for healing. Strengthen me through Your Holy Spirit to treat others as You have treated me. In Jesus' name. Amen.

*Renewal and
restoration are
not luxuries;
they are
essentials.*

—Charles R. Swindoll

Restoration

The return of something to an original or unimpaired condition; bring back into existence.

SEEING THE WORD . . . *RESTORATION*

"Have you ever done this before?" was a question I was often asked during a period when my wife and I were attempting to restore an old house a few years ago.

My pat answer was "No one ever does this twice!" Restoring an aging building is a slow and demanding task.

The house we tackled was built in 1903. It had not been a private residence for nearly 50 years and had sat empty for the 3 years just prior to our project. This house had 14 rooms, plus an attic and a partial basement. There were leaded glass windows, hardwood floors, lovely paneling and moldings throughout—all of which needed a lot of attention.

I learned a fair amount those days about the restoration of things beyond houses, and since then I have often thought about that project in light of God's wonderful promise of spiritual restoration.

"The LORD is my shepherd, I shall not be in want. He makes me lie down in green pastures, he leads me beside quiet waters, he restores my soul" (Ps. 23:1-3).

Note these parallels between God's intentions for us and my experiences restoring "this old house":

1. **Restoration begins with a change of ownership.** It was not possible for us to begin the lofty process of restoration until the "right" was granted by the previous owner. Think of the lives currently in decay and misuse that could be made new if those individuals would give God His rightful place of ownership.

2. **Restoration doesn't happen all at once.** After we had been at work on the house for a few months, people began to ask, "Are you finished yet?" Not only were we not finished, but we had worked long enough to know that this would be a continuing pursuit as long as we lived in that house.

Restoration, be it a house or a life, is not a product but a process—one in which there ought to be some obvious progress, but also a recognition that this is something that continues day after day.

3. **I observed how important it was to clean out the house so that the restoration could begin in earnest.** For weeks a commercial Dumpster sat beside the house as debris, which had accumulated across the years, was cast aside. We cleaned and stripped away that which was decayed and broken beyond repair. Only then could genuine restoration begin.

4. **The goal of restoration is not to change the basic character of the house but to renew it.** There is a keen difference between restoring and remodeling. Restoration tries to recapture the original design and intent of the architect and master builder. God's intentions are to restore and enhance each person's unique personality and character.

5. **Restoration is more pervasive than covering up the past.** Throughout the process the temptation was to paint over, or cover with fabric, rather than to strip away and refinish. True restoration, however, doesn't mask; it renews.

6. **Restoration is costly.** I don't suppose I would have begun the process had I known how much it was ultimately going to cost. Yet things of value always come at a price. "For you know the grace of our Lord Jesus Christ, that though he was rich, yet for your sakes he became poor, so that you through his poverty might become rich" (2 Cor. 8:9).

7. **Some scars remain.** Even after all our work on the house, there were still a few scars—a deep scratch here and there, an irreplaceable pane of glass, or a missing bit of antique molding. These imperfections add to the character of the house. They help tell the story of its years, yet they have ceased to be focal points of the house made new.

HEARING THE WORD . . . *RESTORATION*

It is the nature of things to decay and diminish, and certainly life takes its toll on us from time to time. Yet we take hope in this promise of restoration: "The God of all grace, who called you to his eternal glory in Christ, after you have suffered a little while, will himself restore you and make you strong, firm and steadfast. To him be the power for ever and ever. Amen" (1 Pet. 5:10-11).

It is easier to make new from new, but it is more rewarding and more valuable to make new from old. I'm thankful that God saw potential in our lives and made a commitment to do a new thing in us. The loving hands of the new owner ought to be continually at work restoring us.

United States President John F. Kennedy said, "The time to repair the roof is when the sun is shining." Repairs and restoration should be done as soon as the need is apparent, rather than trying to deal with such things in the midst of inclemency. On the campus where I live and work, we have a set maintenance and replacement schedule. Filters are changed before their efficiency is diminished. Roofs are replaced before the water seeps through. Restoration is a part of the daily upkeep of the campus.

While it may be a bit more difficult to establish such a pattern in every area of life, the principle of having a routine of restoration is sound. I am convinced that this is part of God's created order, beginning with a Sabbath day of rest.

SAYING THE WORD . . . *RESTORATION*

There are many everyday pathways to restoration:
- taking a few moments regularly for silence, meditation, and prayer
- scheduling a day away at a state park, a museum, or a friend's
- taking a walk
- planning a quiet, unhurried meal

Thomas Moore, author of the best-selling books *Care of the Soul* and *Soul Mates,* lived 12 years as a monk. He wrote, "As Monks, we didn't dine; we refected. We never used that word, but the room in which we were, the long hall with tables set on the outer sides only, was called the refectory. The word refers to being remade or refreshed at a meal. Non-monks use a similar word, restaurant, which means to be restored. . . . Thought for food."[1]

We all need spiritual renewal and restoration.

Is there an area of decay in your life that needs to be yielded fully to God so that His grace can bring restoration? It might be
- personal restoration: physical, mental, and emotional, as well as spiritual health. "Simply getting away from linear life, going away in mood or reflection, walking away from the action, or shutting down business as usual: This is all the start of retreat."[2]
- the restoration of a relationship, marriage, friendship, or work relationship

- the restoration of a goal, desire, or dream that has faded or been buried by the routines of life

Identify at least one aspect of your life that you believe needs restoring. Yield that area to God. Commit yourself in prayer to its restoration. Begin to follow the leadership of the One who will enable you to lie down in green pastures, who will lead you to quiet waters. He will restore your soul.

PRAYER

Master Builder, You who made us can surely remake and restore Your creation. Begin that work in me. In Christ's name. Amen.

*Cooperation
is spelled
with two
letters: W-E.*
—George M. Verity

Cooperation

Working or acting together for a common purpose or benefit.

SEEING THE WORD . . . *COOPERATION*

About 20 years ago a man named Thomas Von Beek, a businessman living in Amsterdam, decided that as his company expanded he needed an additional secretary. So he interviewed widely to find a person who would be suitable and decided upon a young lady named Miss Nease.

Miss Nease had only been with the company a few weeks when Mr. Von Beek came to realize that she was an extraordinary worker. She had excellent skills and a wonderful way of responding to everyone. She seemed able to handle all the many situations that arise in the life of a growing business. And most amazingly, she seemed never to run out of energy. She was as fresh in the afternoon and as full of energy as she was in the morning.

Miss Nease worked for Mr. Von Beek for nearly 12 years. At the end of that span of time, she announced that she was going to retire. There were no problems and she was happy, but she decided that she was ready to go on to something else. Von Beek was so grateful to her for all that she had done that he organized a great party in her honor—a going-away party, a retirement party. He invited everyone in the company and many of their customers.

Some parts of the party were to be a surprise, but the greatest surprise of the evening was the one that occurred when the guest of honor arrived.

Mr. Von Beek had said that she did the work of two, but he had no idea that she really was two. At the party he learned for the first time that for 12 years he had actually employed twin sisters.

One of the sisters worked in the mornings and the other in the afternoons, and they split the paycheck.

Think of the teamwork, unity, and communication that must have occurred between those sisters all that time. Their writing styles and work habits had to be similar. The messages given in the morning had to be known by the girl who worked in the afternoon. Any conflicts between them had to be handled in a way as to not affect their work.

Hearing the Word . . . *Cooperation*

Cooperation is fundamental to success in any endeavor in which people must work or live together. No business, organization, or church could effectively function without a spirit of cooperation.

The prophet Amos asks the right question: "Do two walk together unless they have agreed to do so?" (Amos 3:3).

Lefty Gomez was a pitcher for the New York Yankees years ago. At the close of one baseball season in the 1950s when the Yankees had won yet another World Series and Lefty Gomez had pitched a particularly good game, a reporter asked him how he did it. His reply: "I owe my success to clean living and a fast outfield."

In living the Christian life, we understandably put a significant emphasis on "clean living," but let us not forget the strength that comes from a "fast outfield"—a group of men and women who support us, cover for us when we make an error, and encourage us if we perform poorly.

This is the message that Lefty gave: "My success is not possible without the contributions made by my teammates."

It was this realization of the interrelatedness of life that led Augustine in his middle years to write that a wise person will pray for friends because "When we are harassed by poverty, saddened by bereavement, ill and in pain . . . let good people visit us, people who not only rejoice with those who rejoice, but weep with those who weep, and know how to win us to express our own feelings in conversation."

All of life, like the Yankees of the 1950s, is a team sport. We're in this together. We must nurture community and mutual love and support. God exists where there is forgiveness and love and caring and cooperation.

We must care for each other and take up for each other at our points of weakness. "Bear one another's burdens," the Bible says, "and in this way you will fulfill the law of Christ" (Gal. 6:2, NRSV). Too often we fail at this and respond by saying, "That's not my responsibility" or "That's their problem" or by judging one another harshly.

Cooperation is a muscular word. Cooperation isn't always easy. Yet the Christian life and the work of the Church depend in part on the spirit of cooperation and care that is to exist among the people of God.

SAYING THE WORD . . . *COOPERATION*

Many years ago entertainer Jimmy Durante was invited to participate in a special show for veterans. He agreed, but with the condition that he make only a brief appearance before leaving for another engagement.

However, following a short greeting and monologue, rather than leaving, Durante stayed onstage and continued to entertain the audience. The applause grew strong as he continued. Finally, he took a bow and left the stage after performing for over a half hour.

Someone backstage asked him the obvious question: "What happened? I thought you were only going to stay a few minutes."

Durante replied, "Let me show you the reason I stayed." He pointed to two men in the front row, each of whom had lost an arm in the war. One had lost his right arm, the other his left. Together they were able to clap, and that's exactly what they were doing loudly and cheerfully.[1]

PRAYER

God the Father, Son, and Holy Spirit—blessed Trinity—Your grace calls each of us to lives of interdependency, first with You, then with one another. Grant that our first response to others be not the response of competition, but cooperation. Enable us to be quick to see how we might help others and thus show forth Your glory. Give us the wisdom of Solomon to remember that "Two are better than one, because they have a good return for their work: If one falls down, his friend can help him up. But pity the man who falls and has no one to help him up! . . . Though one may be overpowered, two can defend themselves. A cord of three strands is not quickly broken" [Eccles. 4:9-10, 12]. In Jesus' name. Amen.

*I have
chosen the
path of
faithfulness.*

—Ps. 119:30, REB

Faith

Belief in, trust in, and loyalty to, God.

SEEING THE WORD . . . *FAITH*

There were not many things that could have been classified as impossibilities for the ancient Egyptians. One has only to board a bus in the ancient city of Cairo and head out to see the great pyramids to be reminded of the skill, ingenuity, and determination of the people of that culture. The Egyptians could do almost anything they set out to do.

It was with great interest that archaeologists and linguistic scholars worked to decipher the ancient hieroglyphic language of these people. Their language did not use an alphabet as we generally think of an alphabet. This was a language of symbols and pictures in which each item and thought was expressed graphically—pictorially.

Imagine what picture was used to symbolize our word for *impossible.* To express this idea, the Egyptians drew a man's feet on water. A man walking on water—impossible.

I was reminded of that impossibility recently. I went water-skiing. What a sight! What gracefulness! I go skiing about once every five years just to keep my skills sharp.

It's a funny feeling to be floating peacefully in the water, the tips of your skis out in front of you like two sharks talking, when someone calls out, "Are you ready?"

"Ready!"

The rope draws tight, and the peacefulness of the moment is transformed by the surge of a distant engine into a struggle to hang on for dear life. "Just keep your skis in front of you!" someone yells out.

"Easy for *you* to say—you're in the boat!" I say to myself.

What takes only a few seconds seems much longer, yet as I hold steady, the power of the engine soon harmonizes with my struggle, and in that moment I'm "up and off." Skiing is a wonderful experience. It may be as close to walking on the water as we can ever get.

After my initial experience of circling the lake, I was ready to stop but wasn't sure exactly how. Finally I just let go of the rope. As soon as my tie to the power source was gone, I began to sink. After all, walking on the water is impossible—or is it?

HEARING THE WORD . . . *FAITH*

Do you remember the story of Jesus walking on the water toward His disciples who were out on the lake? As the disciples labored against the storm, Jesus came to them across the water. Seeing Him in the distance, Peter called out, "Lord, if it's you . . . tell me to come to you on the water."

"'Come,' he said" (Matt. 14:28-29). With that single word of invitation, Peter responded.

The first step Peter took was to direct his will and intentions toward Christ. His focus was no longer on the storm or his struggle, but on Jesus. What better place to focus when the night is long and the winds are strong?

Evidently Peter felt that where the Master was, there the servant should be as well. So in a moment of faith, Peter stepped overboard and went out across the water to meet the Lord. He did well as long as he kept his eyes on Him.

"But when he saw the wind, he was afraid and, beginning to sink, cried out, 'Lord, save me!'" (Matt. 14:30). Poor Peter panicked. His faith gave way to fear. He lost sight of Christ and focused once more on the difficulties surrounding him. He felt loneliness and the force of the wind on his face and began to sink. Jesus caught him and said, "You of little faith . . . why did you doubt?" (Matt. 14:31).

The Lord's question reveals that it was Peter's faith that had provided the lift. His faith was the "rope" that connected him to the source of power. As long as he believed he could, he could. In the world around us, seeing is believing. But in the kingdom of God, *believing is seeing.*

There may come a time in your life when the waters begin to surge and you hear a voice calling, "Ready?" If you in that instant reply, "Ready!" the power of a distant engine will lift you up, and you, too, will walk on water.

Frederick Buechner points out how prepositions can be very instructive. Consider the difference, he suggests, between *in* and *into.* If we say that a person is "in" medicine, or "in" business, we mean that is what he or she does for a living as a profession. But if we say that someone is "into" something—music, stamp collecting, golf, and so on—this speaks more to the passion and personality of the person.

New Testament Greek speaks of believing "into" rather than simply believing "in." In English this distinction can be seen by using either *in* or no preposition at all.

Believing *in* God is an intellectual proposition and can be almost an abstract proposition. But *believing* God is something else entirely. It doesn't leave you passive, as believing the world is round. It stirs you to action—as believing your house is on fire. Faith is not just believing *in* God. It is a matter of *believing* God—and acting on that belief.

SAYING THE WORD . . . *FAITH*

John G. Payton was a great missionary to the people of the New Hebrides Islands in the Pacific. In his attempt to translate the Gospel of John, he couldn't find a word in their language that adequately expressed the biblical concept of faith.

So he set his efforts aside, waiting for a while until he learned more of the language. Perhaps the right word would come. A few months later a native workman came into his office one day, sat down on a chair, put his feet on another chair, and said to Dr. Payton, "I am resting my entire weight on these two chairs." Now in the language of those people, the phrase "I am resting my entire weight upon" is one single word, and that's the word Payton used to translate our word *faith.*

This meant, for example, that the phrase "Faith in God" was translated by "I am resting my entire weight upon God." This underscores the truth that faith must always have an object. We don't just have faith in a general kind of way; we have faith in a very specific way, faith in someone or something.

Have you rested your entire weight upon God? Are you trusting Him for the unknown areas of life?

Picture a great naval vessel anchored firmly in port. Suddenly an envelope is delivered to the captain on the bridge of the ship. On the outside of the envelope is a departure time, a designated speed, and a set of coordinates of latitude and longitude. The ship begins to come alive as shore leaves are canceled and all supplies are readied.

The destination is unknown, but at the designated time, the great mooring hawsers are released, and the ship slips out of port into the open sea. It's not until it has gone a great distance, not until the ship has reached the designated spot in midocean, that the seal is broken and the final destination revealed.

You may be at a point in your life in which you feel as

though you're sailing under sealed orders. You're not sure at all of your final destination. At such a point in life the message of Scripture is this: "Don't be fearful. Be faithful."

PRAYER

Faithful One, I believe—help my unbelief—that I may keep trying and trusting. I have so few ways to pray, yet You have so many ways to answer, even without my asking. I rest my entire weight upon You. I praise You for Your faithfulness.

From everlasting to everlasting You alone are God. You are all I need. May You be all I want. I fully commit my way to You, confident that You will lead me into paths of righteousness for Your name's sake. In Jesus' name. Amen.

*Grief: no
one escapes.*

—David Switzer

Grief

Deep and poignant distress caused by bereavement, suffering the death of a loved one, or another significant loss.

SEEING THE WORD . . . *GRIEF*

Coats

*I saw him leaving the hospital
with a woman's coat over his arm.
Clearly she would not need it.
The sunglasses he wore could not
conceal his wet face, his bafflement.*

*As if in mockery the day was fair,
and the air mild for December. All the same
he had zipped his own coat and tied
the hood under his chin, preparing
for irremediable cold.*[1]

—Jane Kenyon

HEARING THE WORD . . . *GRIEF*

Grief is a "package" word. It's a bundle of feelings, all miserable, intense, acutely felt. And the pain of grief is more than just sadness or depression. It's sorrow, anxiety, loneliness, fear, guilt, anger, remorse, helplessness—all complex emotions.

Grief takes several forms and works its way through many stages, but at its core it's a profound sense of loss.

It is most often associated with one's response to the death of a loved one, yet it can and does occur in response to other events as well. It's not unusual for a person to experience grief in the following situations:

- a divorce
- a family member moves to a distant location
- the loss of a job
- the breaking of a significant friendship
- the loss of one's health

Grief is woven throughout the fabric of life. No one is immune. It often leaves a person confused, anxious, and depressed. It's experienced physically, emotionally, mentally, and spiritually.

Following the death of his wife, William Armstrong wrote, "Back in the house I moved on leaden feet from chore to chore." All of life is touched when we grieve.

SAYING THE WORD . . . *GRIEF*

Very little in life equips us to grieve effectively and constructively. How does (how should) one grieve? We have no set rules or methods, but some guidelines exist that can be used to aid the process.

1. Accept your pain, that is, don't mask what you're feeling. Stay in touch with yourself through this process. Cry as you need to. Express your feelings. Your feelings must be faced, not denied or repressed.
2. Will to go on.
3. Seek the Lord's help. "You will keep in perfect peace him whose mind is steadfast, because he trusts in you" (Isa. 26:3).

4. Let others help you.
5. Do what has to be done. Go on living as you grieve.
6. Do something specific for someone else: visit a person who is ill or lonely. Be on the giving end of something constructive.
7. Give it time. A day will come when you will be able to remember without pain and tears the person you have lost.
8. Count your blessings—shift your focus.
9. Grieve with hope. "Brothers, we do not want you to be ignorant about those who fall asleep, or to grieve like the rest of men, who have no hope" (1 Thess. 4:13).

Death is a vital part of life itself. "Wherever we turn, we see design and purpose—the hallmark of our creator. It would follow, therefore, that each human being, too, has a purpose, as does every single event in our lives. So even death has a purpose in our lives; even death becomes a tool for leading a more meaningful life."[2]

After all is said and done, however, death is still a devastating experience to those who are left behind. After all the rationalizations, all the explanations, the heart still cries. And it should.

Only when it's dark enough do we begin to see the stars. Even in the midst of grief we know by faith that God in Christ has struck a death blow to death itself. We affirm that there will come a day when death will be no more, when death will be swallowed up in victory, and God will wipe away all tears.

When friends or relatives are grieving for a loved one, don't try to explain; just be there with them. Soothe, console, and weep with them. There's really nothing we can say, for no matter how we might try, we must accept that we often don't understand God's mysterious ways.

After burying three sons, Joseph Bayly wrote:

I was sitting, torn by grief. Someone came and talked to me of God's dealings, of why it happened. Of hope beyond the grave. He talked constantly, he said things I knew were true. I was unmoved except to wish he'd go away. He finally did.

Another came and sat beside me. He just sat beside me for an hour and more, listened when I said something, answered briefly, prayed simply, left. I was moved. I was comforted. I hated to see him go.[3]

PRAYER

Dear Lord, all my life I've tried to avoid as much pain and sorrow as possible. Yet I must face my share. I pray these words of the psalmist: "Be merciful to me, O LORD, for I am in distress; my eyes grow weak with sorrow, my soul and my body with grief. . . . But I trust in you, O LORD; I say, 'You are my God.' My times are in your hands" [Ps. 31:9, 14-15].

Help me to realize that I need not bear my burdens alone. I know that even when I walk through the valley of the shadow of death—You are with me. Help me to trust You when all else seems to be giving way.

I believe—help my unbelief. I have hope because I know You are here and You have borne our griefs and sorrows on the Cross. In Jesus' name I pray. Amen.

*We make a
living by
what we get,
but we make
a life by
what we
give.*

—Winston Churchill

Philanthropy

The generous giving of one's resources in an active effort to promote human welfare; literally "the love of humanity."

SEEING THE WORD . . . *PHILANTHROPY*

James Gordon Kinsley, former president of William Jewell College, tells of making a fund-raising trip to California. The college was in need of a new science building, and he had gone to make a call on an elderly gentleman, an alumnus named Colonel Lee.

Lee was a fascinating man who had served as General Douglas MacArthur's personal pilot in World War II. Then he became vice president of a national airline company. Just after the war he had purchased 2,000 acres of mountain terrain between San Francisco and Los Angeles for nearly nothing. The value of the property, however, had increased substantially across the years and was now valued at nearly $11,000,000. In institutional development terms, that is called "appreciated property," and the one who owns it is called a "prospect." Thus, Dr. Kinsley decided to pay Colonel Lee a visit.

He had been given specific instructions to the colonel's place. As directed, he turned off the coastal highway and entered a winding mountain track spiraling some nine miles up the mountain. The road crossed and recrossed the same rushing creek. It was at first a two-lane asphalt road, then a one-lane asphalt road, then a one-lane gravel road, then a one-lane dirt road that came to a fence with a locked gate. The colonel met Kinsley at the gate, and they drove another half mile in the colonel's four-wheel-drive vehicle to a house he had built with his own hands.

Kinsley describes arriving at the gate:

Now, do you get the picture? Eight and a half miles up the mountain, winding back and forth, two-lane asphalt, one-lane asphalt, one-lane gravel, one-lane dirt, a fence, a locked gate.

And just inside the fence, just inside the locked gate, I was surprised to see a table, some chairs, and three little children sitting there. On the table was a pitcher. And a glass. At the table, hopeful gazes of surprise and appeal. It was, as you surmise, a lemonade stand, and I was a prospect.

"Do you want to buy some lemonade?" a beautiful little blue-eyed girl asked.

Colonel Lee, seeking to be the perfect host, brusquely, even abruptly, said, "No, we don't have time. We are doing business." But, of course, I had to have some lemonade; and so taking care not to offend the $11,000,000 Colonel, I explained that I was thirsty and asked if we could pause just a moment for me to sip a glass. He, still being the perfect host, said, "Of course."

The children were delighted. I asked how much it was. "Ten cents." I didn't have a dime. They did not have change. Business had not been brisk. And so I plunked down a whole dollar, and they poured me a glass, and by this time the pulp was heavy in the glass, and finger prints and probably tongue prints were all around the glass rim, they had been drinking the merchandise through the morning, and I quaffed what was indeed a thick and heady brew, the best lemonade I have drunk, I think, since my own children operated their own lemonade stands.

And because I had been a philanthropist, the littlest girl gave me a wilted mountain rose—I still have it—as a gift. And the littlest boy gave me my choice of petting any of the three scraggly, scrawny dogs lying under the table. My choice.

I went along and did my business with the Colonel, all too unsuccessfully, I fear. He had already disposed of the property among his children, but I came away with treasures. The treasure of his friendship, and the treasure of the lemonade stand at the mountain's peak.[1]

HEARING THE WORD . . . *PHILANTHROPY*

Philanthropy, as the word itself suggests (*philos* means *love,* and *anthrop* means *humanity*), is motivated essentially by love, not by tax breaks or ego.

Generosity becomes difficult only when we forget from where our money and resources come. Every good gift comes from God. All of life is stewardship, not ownership. Once we genuinely accept that all we have is His, it becomes easier to use it as He would use it.

The money you give away is not your own in the first place. The Lord has given it to you to help you experience the joy and the gift of giving. Jesus said, "Give, and it will be given to you. A good measure, pressed down, shaken together and running over, will be poured into your lap. For with the measure you use, it will be measured to you" (Luke 6:38). What a promise!

SAYING THE WORD . . . *PHILANTHROPY*

To leave philanthropy only to the rich is a mistake. It is within the grasp of us all who will give, not for the sake of getting, but to do good, to promote the interests of others and to honor God.

Although you might not be able to give in large amounts, give what you can. The joy is the same.

Have you considered including your church or a favorite charity in your estate planning? Think what good might be done if each person would give just a tenth of his or her estate to help others beyond family.

Take time to involve your children in your charitable giving. Let them help write the checks or review the receipts or place the gift in an envelope or offering container. They know what your car costs, and they see the receipts at the store. They know how much you earn—let them also know how much you give.

Bishop Fulton Sheen suggested that we should not measure our generosity by what we give, but rather by what we have left. Are you satisfied with your level of giving to others? Is God satisfied?

David Livingstone said, "I place no value on anything I possess, except in relation to the Kingdom of God."

PRAYER

O God, You were the first philanthropist. You "so loved the world" that You gave Your only Son that we might be saved. I thank You for this gift, and I pray that You might give me a generous spirit. Help me to love others more than things and to love You more than myself. In Jesus' name I pray. Amen.

*Character cannot be
developed in ease
and quiet. Only
through experiences
of trial and suffering
can the soul be
strengthened, vision
cleared, ambition
inspired, and success
achieved.*

—Helen Keller

Character

The mental, relational, and ethical traits marking and often individualizing a person; moral excellence; integrity.

SEEING THE WORD . . . *CHARACTER*

On the day I was installed as president of the university where I serve, I was given many gifts to commemorate the occasion: from the trustees, the faculty, the students, the alumni association, my friends and family. Among those items was an extended quotation from an essay by Robert Coles, with whom I had studied briefly at Harvard, that had been carefully reproduced, mounted, and framed. It hangs just at the door to my office so that I see it every day. I read it often.

It is taken from a piece Dr. Coles had written first for the *New Oxford Review* and later published in his book of essays titled *Harvard Diary.* The essay is titled "Small Gestures," in which he tells of a student in some distress coming to see him. She had been harassed by a male student and greatly disappointed that someone she had admired and trusted would betray her in such a fashion. He writes:

> She gradually began to realize how much she had learned—without question, the hard way. She began to realize that being clever, brilliant, even what gets called "well-educated," is not to be equated, necessarily, with being considerate, kind, tactful, even plain polite or civil. She began to realize that one's proclaimed social or political views—however articulately humanitarian—are not always guarantors of one's everyday behavior. One can write lofty editorials and falter badly in one's moral life. One can speak big-hearted words, write incisive and thoughtful prose—and be a rather crude, arrogant, smug person in the course of getting through the day.

> Character, my father used to tell me, is what you're like when no one's watching you—or, I guess, when you forget that others are watching.[1]

It is not what one has, nor even what he or she does, that directly expresses the worth of the individual, but what he or she is.

HEARING THE WORD . . . CHARACTER

In one of the later chapters of Robert Wilson's *Character Above All,* a book of biographical essays about 10 United States presidents, Peggy Noonan makes this observation, "In a president, character is everything. A president doesn't have to be brilliant. . . . He doesn't have to be clever; you can hire clever. You can hire pragmatic, and you can buy and bring in policy wonks. But you can't buy courage and decency, you can't rent a strong moral sense."

What she observes about the one who would be president is true of all men and women—"character is everything."[2]

Character is the moral code of personhood. Too much of the success and human relations literature of the past has been "personality-oriented" when it should have been character-based. Yet it is character that ultimately forms the foundation of personality.

Just as a beautiful house that is built on a poor foundation cannot provide a stable and secure habitation, neither can a veneer of personality that seeks to cover or compensate for a weak character provide any sustained happiness or success.

Greek philosopher Hericlitus summed it up in three words: "Character is destiny."

Character is to be understood as the integrated set of a person's most fundamental characteristics and tendencies. Moral perception, moral judgment, attitude formation, emotion, actions, and reactions all blend to produce one's character. Having a good character involves integrity, honesty, patience, courage, kindness, generosity, and a strong sense of personal responsibility.

The world in which we live places great emphasis on the physical, intellectual, and social development of individuals. If only there was the same passion for character development. I often tell parents and students when they are in the process of choosing a college not only to give careful consideration to the academic environment but also to take stock of the spiritual climate of the campus.

I have known many people who have made straight A's in school and then failed at life. The failure resulted not from some academic weakness but from a character flaw. In the end, all education should seek to develop character. Without building a good character, it is impossible to build a truly successful life.

SAYING THE WORD . . . *CHARACTER*

Not long ago I was having dinner with a young man who had just completed his freshman year in college. He is an international student for whom my wife and I had served as surrogate parents. He and I were now looking back on his experience and planning for the year to come. As we talked about possible majors and so on, I said to him, "I believe you can be a great man."

He sat quietly for a moment and then asked me, "What does it take to become a great man?"

I responded by telling him that being a great person begins within. It does not flow from what you do but from who you are—it is rooted in the soil of character.

Character is not a garment to be taken up or laid aside depending upon the prevailing wind or the social climate. It is a person's essential self, which flows from the values, faith, and commitments of the inner person. Ralph Waldo Emerson noted that "What lies behind us and what lies before us are tiny matters compared to what lies within us."

A person of character is one who is trustworthy, reliable, caring, respectful, and fair. In the most fundamental sense, these attributes lie beyond human effort alone. These are most fully realized through the power of God at work within. It is God's grace and the refining work of His Holy Spirit that mold and shape us to be women and men of character. Paul Powell writes, "God is more concerned about our character than our comfort. His goal is not to pamper us physically, but to perfect us spiritually."

When you think of a person of character, what are the characteristics that come to mind?

honesty	dependability
kindness	thoughtfulness
moral integrity	wisdom
truthfulness	faithfulness

Use this list as a mirror. Can you see yourself here? Are these features evident in your life?

Is there one area of character development that you particularly need to strengthen?

In what ways are you actively involved in the character development of your children? "Train up a child in the way he should go: and when he is old, he will not depart from it" (Prov. 22:6, KJV).

PRAYER

Write thy blessed name, O Lord, upon my heart, there to remain so indelibly engraven, that no prosperity, no adversity shall ever move me from thy love. Be thou to me a strong tower of defense, a comforter in tribulation, a deliverer in distress, a very present help in trouble, and a guide to heaven through the many temptations and dangers of this life. Amen.[3]

—Thomas à Kempis

*Memory is
more
indelible
than ink.*

—Anita Loos

Memory

Bringing to mind or thinking of again; the power or process of reproducing or recalling what has been learned or experienced; retention in the mind.

Seeing the Word . . . *Memory*

Several years ago I went to preach a weekend series of services at a church in another state. Assisting in the meeting was a musical trio consisting of two ladies and a gentleman from a neighboring city.

We got off to a good start on Friday evening. The trio sang several selections, and I preached. At the close of the service I went to the back of the church to greet people.

As I was standing there a man walked up to me and said, "Are you the singer?"

"No, I'm the preacher."

"Where ya from?"

"Olivet Nazarene University."

"Oh, I had a boy who went there—never came back."

"Hmm—"

"Do you know where Niles is?"

"More or less," I said.

"I've got a brother who lives there."

And on and on the conversation went for a while until someone else came along and he began to talk with him.

I came back to the church Saturday evening and preached again. At the close of the service I remained near the front of the sanctuary, and a few folks came by to greet me.

Among them was this fellow from the night before. I asked him, "How are you doing this evening?"

He said, "You the singer?"

"No, I'm the speaker."

You can tell I made a great impression on this fellow!

"Where ya from?"

"Olivet Nazarene University."

"I had a boy who went there—never came back. Do you know where Niles is?"

"Yes, unless they moved it since last night."

"I've got a brother who lives there."

I came back the next morning and preached the Sunday morning message, and then as I came to church for the evening service, I slipped into the pastor's study for a few moments of prayer and preparation.

As I was praying, I heard the door open gently. I looked up expecting to see the pastor, but instead there stood this man. He, too, must have been expecting to see the pastor, for he seemed surprised to see me.

He stared a moment and said, shaking his finger, "Are you the singer?"

I said, "No. Write this down—I am the preacher."

"Where ya from?"

"Olivet."

"I had a boy go there—"

"Did he ever come back?" I asked.

"Never came back."

The experience is humorous and sad at the same time. I'm sure this was a wonderful gentleman whose memory had simply become impaired. The incident illustrates, by contrast, what a wonderful thing memory is.

HEARING THE WORD . . . *MEMORY*

Memory *is* a wonderful thing. It is upon our ability to remember that all learning rests. This capacity allows us to function beyond a mere stimulus-response level.

Take away a person's memory, and you take away a great deal of what it means to be that person. Such is the tragedy of Alzheimer's disease and other forms of senility.

Remembering gives us the ability
to relive days gone by,
to recapture special moments in life,
to recall friends and family
from a former day.

Memory can be stimulated by the will or by the moment. You hear a song on the radio and, through that music, a door of memory is opened. You remember an event when you were younger and that song was playing.

Memory can be a wonderful thing.

But our memory can also haunt us. I know several people who can't move on in life because they are plagued by bad memories.

In one sense the past is dead and gone, never to be repeated—over and done with. But in another sense it's not done with at all or, at least, it's not done with us.

Every person we have ever known, every place we have ever seen, everything that has ever happened to us is retained deep within our memory. Some of it we can recall at will. Much of it we cannot.

Then there are those moments when, whether we like it or not, our memory is triggered and somewhat suddenly we are overtaken once more by our past. Sometimes it doesn't take much to bring it back to the surface.

On occasion these are moments of serendipitous delight, but at other times a bad memory springs upon us, and we're engulfed in guilt, anger, or depression.

What should happen when the bad memories surface—the guilt memories? Some people just try to forget. "Why dwell on the past?" they say to themselves. But bad memories pushed back into the secret places of ourselves can do a lot of harm.

We often wish that our past was past, but it's not. It lingers. It continues to live right on the edge of the present, sometimes casting its shadow across our pathway.

Pushing the past away does not resolve it.

Saying the Word . . . *Memory*

"Burying our past," says Henri Nouwen, "is like turning our back on our best teacher."

When an unpleasant memory returns, don't just suppress it or ignore it—face it. Hold it up to the light of the here-and-now, and commit it fully to God. His grace can heal the past. His love can wash away the stain of regret or bitterness that tends to infect the present.

God has a divine capacity both to remember and to forget. He will always remember you and be mindful of your needs—but He is quick to forget that which has been forgiven, and His grace can enable you to do the same.

When your sins are forgiven, they are forgotten: "As far as the east is from the west, so far has he removed our transgressions from us" (Ps. 103:12).

What God forgives, He forgets. This doesn't happen as a result of a memory lapse on the part of God. He *chooses* not to remember. For the sake of love He forgets. This kind of forgetting is what the Bible calls "forgiveness."

God forgets what you have done so that He might never forget you. The psalmist David said it like this: "Remember, O Lord, your great mercy and love, for they are from of old. Remember not the sins of my youth and my rebellious ways; according to your love remember me, for you are good, O LORD" (Ps. 25:6-7).

Tomorrow's memory depends upon today's impressions. One should seek actively to fill the reservoir of memory with good things. Memory is a gallery in which you can collect that which is beautiful and good. It is a bank account in which you may deposit treasures to be reclaimed at a later time and from which you can withdraw joy, encouragement, faith, and hope.

The quality of your life will help determine both your memories in days to come and other people's memory of you as well. Some memories are realities that are better than anything that can ever happen to you again. Italo Svevo said, "God created memory so that we might have roses in December."

Too often we dwell more on negative thoughts than on those of God's many blessings. Our lives are far more confused and complicated than they need to be. A quiet reminder to stop negative thinking and remember God can make a significant difference. Such is the value of a regular devotional time and a consistent pattern of worship. God will strengthen us and take away our fears if we remember to remember Him.

There are two ways of remembering. One is to make an excursion from the living present into the past, recalling things past. The second is to summon a memory from the past into the presence, so that that moment or person is present and living once again. When Jesus said, "Do this in remembrance of me" (Luke 22:19), He was pledging His living presence to be with us whenever we take time to remember.

In his classic novel *One Hundred Years of Solitude,* Colombian author Gabriel Garcia Marquez tells of a village where people were afflicted with a strange plague of forgetfulness. It was a kind of contagious amnesia. Moving slowly through the population of the village, the plague caused people to forget the names of even the most common everyday objects.

One young man, yet unaffected, tried to limit the damage by putting labels on everything: "This is a table." "This is a window." "This is a cow; it has to be milked every morning." And at the entrance to the town, on the main road, he put up two large signs. One read "The name of our village is Macondo," and the other sign, larger, read, "God exists." The thing he wanted to be sure to remember and to help others remember above all else was that God exists.[1]

Perhaps in the course of time you may forget much of what you have learned and experienced. Dates and names and places may fade. Some skills, if not used, you may in time forget.

All of that forgetting may not matter too much. But if we forget God, if we forget the One to whom we belong, if we let our hearts get cluttered and crowded and cramped, if we lose our way spiritually, then no other amount of re-membering will make much difference.

PRAYER

Holy One, there is something I wanted to tell you, but there have been errands to run, bills to pay, arrangements to make, meetings to attend, friends to entertain, washing to do . . . and I forgot what it is I wanted to say to you, and mostly I forget what I'm about or why.

O God, don't forget me, please, for the sake of Jesus Christ.[2]

—Ted Loder

*For the grace
of God that
brings
salvation has
appeared to
all men.*

—Paul (Titus 2:11)

race

Unmerited divine favor and assistance.

SEEING THE WORD . . . *GRACE*

In a small parish cemetery in Olney, England, stands a granite tombstone with the following inscription:

> John Newton, clerk, once an infidel and Libertine, a servant of slavers in Africa, was, by the rich mercy of our Lord and Savior Jesus Christ, preserved, restored, pardoned, and appointed to preach the Faith he had long labored to destroy.

This epitaph, written by Newton himself, describes the dramatic conversion and ministry of one of the great preachers and hymn writers of the 18th century.

John Newton was born in London in 1725. His father was a seaman. His mother was a godly woman who died when John was only 7. He went to sea himself at the age of 11.

As he came of age, his life was marked by debauchery and rebellion. He was heavily involved in the slave trade between Africa and the New World, and he lived a wicked life.

On March 10, 1748, while returning to England from Africa during a particularly stormy voyage, Newton began reading from Thomas à Kempis's book *The Imitation of Christ.* The message of this book, which revived in his thinking the influence of his godly mother, plus the frightening experiences at sea were used by the Holy Spirit to sow seeds that would lead to Newton's spiritual conversion.

As he grew spiritually, he left his old life, returned to England, and became a strong and effective crusader against slavery. He married and settled into a stable, godly life with his wife and family.

In 1755 he was appointed tide surveyor at Liverpool. It was there that he met John and Charles Wesley and George Whitefield. They encouraged him to prepare for the ministry.

In 1764 Newton was ordained. In 1779 he was invited to the post of rector of St. Mary's Woolnoth Church in London. Of this appointment he wrote: "That one of the most ignorant, most miserable, most abandoned of slaves, should be plucked from his exile on the coast of Africa, and at length be appointed minister of the chief parish, in the chief city of the world; that he should here testify, not only of God's grace, but stand up as a monument to it; and record it in his history, his preaching, and his writings to the world at large, is a fact that I can never sufficiently thank God for."

Throughout his life and ministry, John Newton never ceased to marvel at the grace of God, which had so dramatically changed his life. This became the dominant theme of his preaching and writing. Not long before his death a spokesman for the church suggested that he consider retirement because of ill health. Newton replied, "What?

Shall the old African blasphemer stop while he can still speak?" On another occasion he proclaimed, "My memory is nearly gone, but I remember two things: that I am a great sinner and that Christ is a great Savior!"[1]

Newton wrote hundreds of hymns. One stands out among them as the most representative expression of his life and testimony. This is his original version:

Amazing grace! how sweet the sound
That saved a wretch like me!
I once was lost, but now am found;
Was blind, but now I see.

'Twas grace that taught my heart to fear,
And grace my fears relieved.
How precious did that grace appear
The hour I first believed!

Thro' many dangers, toils, and snares
I have already come.
'Tis grace hath brought me safe thus far,
And grace will lead me home.

The Lord has promised good to me;
His word my hope secures.
He will my shield and portion be
As long as life endures.

Yes, when this flesh and heart shall fail
And mortal life shall cease,
I shall possess within the veil
A life of joy and peace.

The earth shall soon dissolve like snow,
The sun forbear to shine;
But God, who called me here below,
Will be forever mine.

> When we've been there ten thousand years,
>   Bright, shining as the sun,
> We've no less days to sing God's praise
>   Than when we'd first begun.

HEARING THE WORD . . . *GRACE*

In the New Testament the word *grace* is of central importance. It is the key word of Christianity. Grace is what the gospel is all about, for we are saved by grace through faith (see Eph. 2:8).

Thomas Oden writes, "Grace is God's way of empowering the bound will and healing the suffering spirit. The unmerited blessing of God is being offered to all who are alienated from their true selves."[2]

We of the human race, however, have shown a remarkable resourcefulness in our attempts to provide a substitute for grace. We have placed our trust in possessions, in power, in reputation, and our common intellect. But no matter how much we have or who we are or what we know, we can never gain nor merit what is freely given by God. God is gracious, not because of who we are but because of who He is. God is love, and love must be expressed. By grace we are the objects of His love.

The attraction of grace lies in the understanding that it is something you can never get but only be given. One cannot earn it, deserve it, or bring it about. One can only receive it and be thankful.

Grace is God's undeserved favor, His unmerited love. Grace is God acting in spontaneous goodness to save sinners—loving the unlovely. Though we possess nothing within us to merit God's favor, He favors us nonetheless.

Frederick Buechner suggests that grace is the "crucial eccentricity" of the Christian faith: "There is nothing *you* have to do. There is nothing you *have* to do. There is nothing you have *to do.* There is only one catch. Like any gift, the gift of grace can be yours only if you reach out and take it. And, of course, being able to reach out and take it is a gift too."[3]

This amazing grace of God does not, however, destroy human freedom. God knocks upon the door to our life but does not break it down. He calls, but we must answer. Grace appeals to our free will as the Holy Spirit works to awaken our spirit to God's grace. Through grace the Spirit illuminates the mind, encourages the will, and guides the senses so that we may respond to God's offer of salvation.

Grace is the liberating force that sets human nature free from its bondage to sin. Augustine used the phrase "the captive free will" to describe humanity's condition under the heavy influence of sin. He taught that grace is able to liberate the human will from this influence. He also saw grace as the healer of human nature. The only "cure" for sin was salvation by the grace of God in Christ. Grace functions also as a spiritual energy that enables the child of God to live a righteous life.

SAYING THE WORD . . . *GRACE*

If you're buying a house and arrange a mortgage with a financial institution, your payments are probably due on the first of each month. Should you fail to make a payment on that date, you may have until the 15th to get it in before receiving a penalty. This extra time is called a "grace period."

Christians, too, have a grace period. But it's different from what the financial institution extends to its mortgage holders, which is not grace in the full sense of the term— merely a temporary reprieve. The financial institution's favor comes to an end on the 15th. Full payment is then demanded, or a penalty will be added.

By contrast, what we owe God by way of indebtedness for our sins has been fully paid by Jesus' death on the Cross. In the Book of Romans the Bible says, "Where sin abounded, grace abounded much more" (Rom. 5:20, NKJV).

Furthermore, He imparts to us by His Spirit both the desire and the strength to do His will. That makes our entire life a continuous extension of divine favor, which we appropriate by faith. "So then, just as you received Christ Jesus as Lord, continue to live in him" (Col. 2:6).

Every day is a grace period.

But some might say that if God's grace gives us freedom from sin's penalty, then we can live as we please. No! Grace does not give us license—it calls us to responsibility. Grace does not offer freedom to sin; it offers freedom from sin. The imparting of grace brings a new life that creates within us a desire to please God and gives us the power to overcome evil. "For the grace of God that brings salvation has appeared to all men. It teaches us to say 'No' to ungodliness and worldly passions, and to live self-controlled, upright and godly lives in this present age, while we wait for the blessed hope—the glorious appearing of our great God and Savior, Jesus Christ, who gave himself for us to redeem us from all wickedness and to purify for himself a people that are his very own, eager to do what is good" (Titus 2:11-14).

The Christian's grace period puts us on the receiving end of God's unending favor. It calls us to live in such a way that we bring glory to God.

God's grace is not static but active. It is a spiritual energy at work in us and for us. Grace is God's love in action empowering us for good.

The life of grace is one of freedom. You who accept by faith the saving grace of God are freed from the necessity of trying to earn your salvation by being good enough. There is no need for you to go through life worrying that you're not good enough for God. His grace does not depend upon your goodness. In fact, it is His grace that has set you free from the tyranny of the Law (always striving to be "good enough").

Yet the good news is that the power of His grace also sets you free from sin's domination, for the grace of God enables the believer to live the Christlike life. It is grace that breaks the bondage of fear and spiritual insecurity, for "if

God is for us, who can be against us?" (Rom. 8:31). "The Spirit himself testifies with our spirit that we are God's children" (v. 16).

PRAYER

O God of grace, I pause to look back upon my life—to see who I was before You rescued me, to ponder where I might be, what I might have become with Your grace. You have transformed me and set me free. Fill my heart with thankful praise as I meditate upon my sins forgiven, my shame unpublished.

I thank You for Your love, mercy, and grace. I thank You that You are my Father and that I am Your child.

May I now use these gifts of new life and freedom to be an instrument of Your grace to others. In Christ's name. Amen.

NOTES

HOPE

1. Lillian Eichler Watson, ed., *Light from Many Lamps* (New York: Simon and Schuster, 1988), 62-66.

2. Thomas à Kempis, *The Imitation of Christ* (New York: Hippocrene Books, 1986), The Third Book, Chap. 48, 203.

GRATITUDE

1. John C. Bowling, "Psalm for a Pickpocket," *Herald of Holiness,* February 1994, 46.

2. Quoted in a 1988 unpublished sermon by Bruce Theilman, senior pastor of Fourth Presbyterian Church, Pittsburgh.

ADVERSITY

1. Hurbert Nelson, *Daily Readings from Spiritual Classics,* ed. Paul Ofstedal (Minneapolis: Augsburg Fortress, 1990), 313-27.

2. à Kempis, *Imitation of Christ,* The First Book, chap. 12, 20.

PRAYER

1. Richard Foster, quoted in "Words for Quiet Moments," *Catholic Digest,* May 1996, 90.

COMPASSION

1. Response given by Margaret Mead in a question-and-answer session at the National Association of Religious Education annual conference, November 1978, Chase Park Plaza Hotel, St. Louis.

2. Lucinda Vardey, comp., *Mother Teresa: A Simple Path* (New York: Ballantine Books, 1995), 90.

PERSEVERANCE

1. Quoted in Suzy Platt, ed., *Respectfully Quoted: A Dictionary of Quotations* (New York: Barnes and Noble Books, 1993), 255.

2. "Down but Not Out," *Runner's World,* August 1991, 10.

CHURCH

1. "The Church Itself" in J. Kenneth Grider, *A Wesleyan-Holiness Theology* (Kansas City: Beacon Hill Press of Kansas City, 1994), 469.
2. Quoted in Reuben P. Job and Norman Shawchuck, *A Guide to Prayer for Ministers and Other Servants* (Nashville: Upper Room, 1983), 88.

TRUST

1. Frederick Buechner, *Listening to Your Life* (San Francisco: HarperCollins, 1992), 326.
2. Ibid.
3. Bill Hybels, *Seven Wonders of the Spiritual World* (Dallas: Word, 1988), 53.

ATTITUDE

1. Anne Frank, *The Diary of a Young Girl* (Garden City, N.Y.: Doubleday, 1952), 239.
2. John Baillie, *A Diary of Private Prayer* (New York: Charles Scribner and Sons, 1949), 24.

TIME

1. Quoted in Charles Swindoll, *The Quest for Character* (Portland, Oreg.: Multnomah Press, 1987), 74.
2. Charles Swindoll, *Come Before Winter* (Portland, Oreg.: Multnomah Press, 1985), 24-25.

AGE

1. Frederick Buechner, *The Longing for Home: Recollections and Reflections* (San Francisco: Harper San Francisco, 1996), 1-2.

WORK

1. Elton Trueblood, *Your Other Vocation* (New York: Harper and Row, 1952), 57.
2. Charles Swindoll, *Life Beyond the Daily Grind II* (Waco, Tex.: Word Publishing, 1988), 415.
3. Robert Slocum, *Ordinary Christians* (Waco, Tex.: Word, 1986), 154-68.
4. Ibid., 155-56.
5. Ibid., 159.
6. Ibid., 162.
7. Ibid., 163.

8. Ibid., 167.
9. Ibid., 66.
10. Ibid.

Charity

1. Vardey, *Mother Teresa,* xi.
2. Ibid., 79.

Reconciliation

1. William H. Hinson, *Solid Living in a Shattered World* (Nashville: Abingdon Press, 1985), 121-22.

Restoration

1. Thomas Moore, *Meditations* (New York: HarperCollins, 1994), 47.
2. Ibid., 5.

Cooperation

1. Alice Bray, comp., *Stories for the Heart* (Gresham, Oreg.: Vision House, 1996), 46.

Grief

1. "Coats," copyright 1996 by the Estate of Jane Kenyon. Reprinted from *Otherwise: New and Selected Poems* with the permission of Graywolf Press, St. Paul, Minn.
2. Menachem Mendal Schneerson, *Toward a Meaningful Life: The Wisdom of the Rebbe,* adapted by Simon Jacobson (New York: William Morrow and Co., 1995), 123.
3. Quoted in Bray, *Stories for the Heart,* 219.

Philanthropy

1. From a speech given by Dr. James Gordon Kingsley to the 15th annual meeting of the Clearinghouse for Midcontinent Foundations, June 15, 1990. Published in Dr. James Gordon Kingsley, *Conversations with Leaders for a New Millennium: Addresses in a College Community* (Liberty, Mo.: William Jewell Press, 1991), 50-51. Used by permission.

Character

1. Robert Coles, "Small Gestures," in *Harvard Diary: Reflections on the Sacred and the Secular* (New York: Crossroad Publishing Co., 1990), 111-12.
2. Robert A. Wilson, ed., *Character Above All* (New York: Simon and Schuster, 1995), 202.

3. Quoted in Job and Shawchuck, *A Guide to Prayer,* 98-99.

MEMORY

1. Harold Kushner, *Who Needs God* (New York: Summit Books, 1989), 207.

2. Ted Loder, *Guerrillas of Grace: Prayers for the Battle* (San Diego: LuraMedia, 1984), 60-61.

GRACE

1. Wilbur Konkel, *Hymn Stories: The Story Behind Some of the Greatest Hymns of the Church* (Salem, Ohio: Schmul Publishing Co., 1986), 64-67.

2. Thomas C. Oden, *The Transforming Power of Grace* (Nashville: Abingdon Press, 1993), 15.

3. Buechner, *Listening to Your Life,* 289.